D0094288

HOW TO BECOME A
VETERINARIAN

WHAT THEY DO, HOW TO TRAIN, DAILY LIFE AS VET, IS IT REALLY THE RIGHT CAREER FOR YOU?

SUSANNA LEE

© Copyright 2019 - All rights reserved. Legal Notice: This book is copyright protected. This book is only for personal use. You cannot amend, distribute, sell, use, quote or paraphrase any part, or the content within this book, without the consent of the author or publisher.

Dedicated to our heroic vets who go above and beyond the call of duty to ease the suffering of animals.

Also dedicated to young people around the world who aspire to follow in their footsteps.

Contents

Introduction

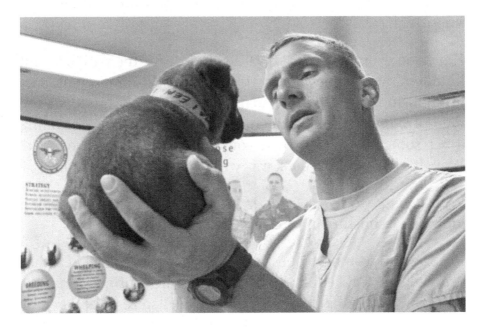

Have you ever come down with an illness or injured yourself while playing and you had to visit a doctor? Well, I'm sure you must have at some point. Animals, too, suffer from certain illnesses and may get hurt sometimes.

But, just as you sometimes get sick and require the skills of a doctor, your pet also does. Animals are not so different from us. Knowing this, don't you think it's right that they have a trained and licensed doctor to look after them?

For health, hygiene and other reasons, we cannot expect animals to share the same hospitals and doctors as humans. As a result, there ought to be a group of individuals who have been equipped with the right skills needed to cater especially for animals.

These heroes are called veterinarians.

From rats to pigs and even snakes, vets can do check-ups and perform surgeries on a variety of animals. They work as hard as the doctors who treat humans, and are equally as important.

Have you ever visited a vet? Did you observe the patience and kindness with which they treated every animal that was brought to them? Did this spark a curiosity in you about the field of veterinary medicine and make you consider becoming a vet someday? If yes, then you are in luck. Why, you ask? Well, it's because this book was written with you in mind.

Wanting to work as a vet is a worthwhile and rewarding ambition to nurture in your mind.

But I'm sure you have questions. Some of which may be, what exactly does it take for a person to become a professional vet and how long is the process? Can anyone aspire to be a vet, or is it best for people with particular personality types? How much do vets make, and what is a typical working day like?

This book offers a helping hand to guide you in discovering the answers to these questions. Veterinary medicine is a very rewarding career path. It is a field of heroes, though without capes and masks, who sacrifice their time and use their special abilities to make animals feel better. They do this each and every day, and even though animals don't speak, their regained health and renewed liveliness show how thankful they are.

It is fantastic that you have entertained the idea of joining the league of super vets to fight the forces that try to make animals weak, unhealthy or sad.

Unlike some other books, this is one you can always come back to regardless of how long ago you've read it. The information contained here will serve you now, and for as many times as you choose to go through its chapters. Veterinary medicine can never have enough people working to make sure the well-being of animals is ensured.

I have made every effort to make sure this book is enjoyable, informative, answers your questions and paints an accurate picture of this unique field of healthcare.

Susanna Lee

Chapter 1

Vets: Who Are They?

Anyone who has been trained and certified to treat animals — to prevent, cure and manage their health-related issues — can be called a veterinarian. This is often shortened to "vet" because it is an easier way to pronounce the name.

Usually, we imagine that vets only have to deal with pets, but these animal doctors are in fact trained to also treat farm animals and even wild animals. They diagnose animals to determine the cause of their discomforts, prescribe treatments and, should an animal die, perform autopsies to reveal what caused its death.

Vets, indirectly, also get to save humans sometimes. Doctors of veterinary medicine have been known to identify and cure diseases in animals which could be contracted by humans — diseases that may have caused an epidemic.

Vets are invaluable members of the healthcare world who carry out their duties with diligence and dignity. Their efforts every day go into making the world a much safer and happier place for both animals and humans to live in.

Like every other job, veterinary practice does come with some challenges. Every day for a vet is not a breeze — we'll talk about this in a later chapter. But along with the challenges, it's the smiles, light-heartedness and little victories that make all the difference for many vets around the world.

A Short History Of Veterinary Practice

Different sources place the earliest records of veterinary practice at different times in history. Some even go as far back as 9000 BC, but no one can state for sure the exact time veterinary medicine was born or the first person to practice it.

One man, though, is credited with popularizing healthcare for animals. His name was Urlugaledinna - can you pronounce that! He lived around 3000 BC in Babylonia and was recorded in history books as "an expert in healing animals". Little more is known about him, but we can tell from the historic writings that he became very famous for treating and curing animals with a variety of ailments.

Still, there were no schools at the time for the study of veterinary medicine nor was it considered an actual practice. Many more years had to go by before a school was finally established in Lyons, France, by Claude Bourgelat. This was in 1762 AD, and it was called Lyon Veterinary School.

It opened the path for the creation of even more schools to equip individuals with veterinary knowledge. The year 1765 saw Claude Bourgelat establishing Alfort School in Paris. In 1791, the Royal Veterinary College was founded in London. A team led by Granville Penn spearheaded it. These developments meant that veterinary medicine was officially considered to be a profession. As for which type of animals were treated by these newly created vets, it may surprise you to know that domestic animals and livestock were not, at first, the focus.

Before cars, buses, motorbikes and other types of modern transportation, humans still had the need to travel from one location to another. Some travels involved long distances, which would have been impossible for any human being to attempt. Horses were the helpers of that age. And because they were so often used to cover treacherous terrain and miles and miles in distances, it was not uncommon for a horse to suffer serious injuries or fall ill. It was up to the vets to treat them.

After a few years, veterinarians broadened their scope to include livestock. It was not until much later that pets such as cats and dogs were added to the group of animals that were helped by vets.

Why We Need Vets

Now that you know some of the history of vets and you know what they do, it is easier to understand how their jobs are invaluable to societies. But what if you were asked to give reasons for why they are so important? How many can you list right now? Below are seven points to help you.

They bring healing to animals and relief to their owners

A world without veterinarians is one where animals would have to suffer a great deal. What works to relieve the pains of humans and cure their illnesses is not guaranteed to work on animals. Pet and livestock owners can, on their own, only guess at what would soothe the suffering of their animals. This guessing can go wrong sometimes, and may even prove fatal.

Licensed and practicing vets have spent years learning the anatomy of various animals in detail. They know how animals are likely to react to different things and can make informed judgments as to the source of an animal's discomfort. Since animals cannot speak, it is tough to communicate your intentions to them. This is even worse when they are sick.

Besides the academic qualifications expected of every vet, they are usually patient and have a sincere appreciation for animals. This makes them the best people to care for your pet when it falls ill. The animals get comprehensive medical care in a manner that is not mere troubleshooting, and their owners have peace of mind.

They enlighten us

A large number of us would still be in the dark on how to care for animals were it not for veterinarians. Along with treating animals, they also advise owners on what to do — for example, there are some foods that are harmful to animals and should be avoided. If you own certain breeds of dog, you will need to add vitamins to their diet to stop them from becoming ill. Vets share this critical advice and information, which is often life-saving.

They help us make hard decisions

Many pet owners are so attached to their animals that they might delay making the right choices, or go with what is more comfortable for the animal in the short term.

Imagine you have noticed your dog showing increasing signs of weakness and disinterest, and you take it to a vet. After tests, let's say that it was discovered that your pet is suffering from an ailment whose cure would require surgery. The catch here is that the chances of something serious happening to your dog as a result of this surgery are so high that the procedure is rarely attempted.

On the other hand, your pet's life may be at risk if you do not agree to the surgery. How would it make you feel to be faced with such a decision?

Sometimes, even surgery is not enough to save an animal's life. The vet may suggest euthanasia (ending a life to relieve pain and suffering), but it is up to the pet owner to decide if they should go through with it. Vets are trained to assist people in making very difficult decisions on what would be best for their animals.

They inspire us

You may think that some vets only enter the profession because of the financial rewards or status. But you also have to consider that veterinary medicine is, by most standards, not the highest paying job out there. And even if it were, the process to become certified as a veterinarian requires a lot of hard work and takes quite a bit of time. Most people who are only pursuing money would not choose this career path.

Vets are genuinely passionate about their jobs and they get great satisfaction from improving the quality of life of animals. It is inspiring and humbling that anyone would dedicate a large portion of their life to becoming educated in helping animals and then spend the rest of their career serving that mission.

They prevent epidemics

Even though "proper scientists" would not take her seriously at first, veterinary pathologist Tracey McNamara was the first to solve the puzzle of birds falling from the sky in 1999. She suggested West Nile virus as the culprit for the birds raining down and for people dying from encephalitis (swelling of the brain) as a result. She was proved right!

Throughout history, there has always existed a connection between us and the animal life around us — we need them for food, transport, work and companionship. The last reason is more significant than ever now that so many families have taken to adopting animals as members of their families. Animals have had years to build up antibodies which fight particular diseases. The same is often not true for humans. Unfortunately, when we contract some of these diseases from animals, they can be fatal.

Veterinarians are at the forefront of the battle against pandemics. They usually are the first to identify certain illnesses that have the potential of spreading from animals to the human population, and that could prove extremely harmful if not fatal. Aren't they just fabulous? When next you see a vet, remember that you are looking at an actual superhero!

They help to create animal models

After dedicating years of studying to the anatomy of animals, there isn't a better candidate than a qualified vet to build an accurate model of any animal. Schools, robotics companies and biological companies are just a few of the organizations that require veterinarians to create models of animals which include every organ, muscle and other body part.

Beyond the anatomy of animals, vets also know in detail why and how animals behave the way they do. Since their intellect is devoted to animal science, they are the perfect source for answers on anything animal related. What's better, the majority of them are only too glad to answer whatever questions you might have about your pet.

They are responsible for increased productivity in livestock

First, what is responsible for livestock performing poorly in any respect? The most likely answer for this is disease. If a bacterium strikes an animal, they might exhibit symptoms that include tiredness or loss of movement. Livestock is reared for several reasons, some of which are to provide meat, milk, fur, wool and leather, and for sports.

Owners lose money when their animals do not fulfill the purpose for which they are kept, and they turn to vets to inquire about the reasons for this decrease in productivity. Our favorite heroes, the veterinarians, do not only give accurate answers to the livestock owners, but they also step in and fix the problem.

The Different Types of Vets

Specialist Veterinarians

Immediately after their four years of veterinary school, qualified animal doctors can set up their practices and start helping animals.

However, some are not satisfied with this and train further to become specialized. This usually requires at least one year of internship or hands-on experience working in a particular veterinary specialty. After this, there could be a residency program that could last as long as three years.

These special vets learn large volumes of information related to their area of specialization before taking a final board exam. They receive diplomas which certify them in that specialty after they pass the exam. Below are a few of the many veterinary specializations.

- Surgery

- Toxicology

- Microbiology

- Pathology

- Pharmacology

- Ophthalmology

- Dentistry

- Radiology

- Preventive medicine

- Poultry veterinary

- Nutrition

- Anesthesia

Marine Life Veterinarians

Fishes, large and small, and other water creatures need care, too. Like land animals, they are susceptible to diseases. Human life on Earth would find it very hard to keep existing if marine life was driven to extinction. They not only serve as food, but keep water bodies clean, too. These, and many more reasons, are why some veterinarians have focused their practice on animals that have made oceans and rivers their home.

Feline Veterinarians

Largely because they've got a soft spot for cats, these vets only treat cases involving the feline species of the animal kingdom. They also gain a lot of experience in this area, which makes them better suited to handle cat cases than vets who generalize their practice. Cat owners often prefer vets whose niche involves nothing besides cats.

Canine Veterinarians

Like their feline veterinarian counterparts, these specialists are devoted to just one species — dogs. This may stem from a personal fondness for dogs or because they want to enter a popular niche for their practice. Whatever the reason, we are grateful to these men and women who help make our dogs the lively and energetic animals we have come to adore.

Mobile Veterinarians

They are always available on call and do not find it a bother to visit your home and check your pet for the source of their discomfort. These vets may not have a permanent clinic location, but move about in their cars with their kits or mobile clinics. Instead of waiting for their clients to come to them, they bring help to their door upon request. All you have to do is call and explain the condition of your pet or livestock.

Wildlife Veterinarians

If you watch National Geographic or any other television channel or documentary that features wildlife, then you have most likely seen these vets. Dressed appropriately for the wild, they treat injured and sick animals. You will also find them working to prevent certain creatures from going extinct. They feed, heal, tag and keep track of these animals. They make it their responsibility to nurture these animals back to good health and a sizeable population.

Equine Veterinarians

These are another group of vets who are devoted to a single type of animal. They take care of horses and make sure they are in top shape to perform optimally. This practice is one of the oldest branches of veterinary medicine and the first to be recognized as a profession. Although horses are no longer in use as much as they used to be, their participation in sports and parades means they still need the care of skilled vets.

Academic Veterinarians

You already know that vets have to spend a lot of time learning how to perform their job correctly. This means that someone has to be there to pass this knowledge on to them. Instead of practicing, some trained vets choose to be the ones who equip upcoming veterinarians with the information and skills they require to make a positive difference in the lives of animals. They are no less heroes than practicing vets. The quality and skill of any animal doctor is dependent greatly on the efforts of their teachers.

Avian Veterinarians

We keep parrots as pets, rear turkeys for Thanksgiving and enjoy the colors of a macaw in flight. Birds are beautiful and, mostly, delicate creatures. They need our help sometimes to stay healthy and chirpy. There is also a significant chance of humans getting infected with diseases passed on from birds because we pet, feed and eat them. Avian veterinarians are not only skilled at ensuring the good health of birds, but they also contribute to the continued welfare of humans.

Companion Animal Veterinarians

All the other vets in this list are either focused on particular animals or treat all kinds of species. Companion animal veterinarians are pet-centered. They are here to make sure the animals that are also your companions stay in good health. They promote a happier relationship between pets and their owners and have great skills in passing on knowledge and advice to pet owners. For this specialization you need to like humans beings as much as you love animals!

Chapter 2

Training to be a Vet

Since we have mentioned how veterinarians must train long and hard before they can be licensed to practice, it is only right that we now explore what it takes to get there.

In the time it takes to be thoroughly trained — which could last as long as eight years including college, internship and residency — a few things are required of a vet in training. There are recommended books they have to buy and read, courses they must take, lectures they cannot avoid and vocational training they should ideally volunteer for.

You may have pondered this question, but there are also some personality traits that are more suited to the veterinary profession than others. Here is what you need to know to become a vet.

Qualifications You Will Need

Professional qualifications validate your skills as a vet. This means they make people trust your claim to be an expert in treating animals. You also run the risk of getting arrested or sanctioned for practicing veterinary medicine without them! So proper qualifications are an absolute must-have requirement.

Let us now look at the qualifications that are expected of veterinarians.

- You must have attended high school (also called secondary school in Europe) and taken your SAT/ACT (GCSEs and A-Levels in the UK). No university will even look twice at a candidate's application if it does not include their performance in these exams. It is not something you can skip or take lightly.

  If it is your dream to be a vet someday, then failure in mathematics or science subjects such as biology and chemistry will not do you any favors. Veterinary medicine is as much a science as any other, and it requires its students to have mastered, at least to a point, core science subjects such as biology and chemistry.

  If you are so determined to join the veterinary profession that you put every distraction aside, you might find that these subjects aren't so tough after all. You only need to be focused and consistent in your studying.

- Next, you will have to decide on a university (see the list at the back of this book for some of the top veterinary schools). When you have been accepted by any of these, you can't slouch in your studies. Your future in a college for veterinary medicine, and any other dreams you might have relating to this field of medicine, rides on how effectively you spend your time in the university.

  Again, core science subjects like mathematics and chemistry will be crucial in getting colleges to consider you as a strong applicant. Give your best to every subject — especially core related subjects such as biology and zoology. Be smart with your study choices.

  Alongside choosing the right subjects, you will have to maintain a minimum grade point average (GPA) of 3.5. Veterinary schools prefer candidates who can show this grade point in their applications. Achieving this requires focus, commitment and, above all, consistency in your studies.

  Participate in school-approved extracurricular activities and, after you have graduated, volunteer at vet clinics. These activities will boost you to the top of the pile of applications sent in to vet school. I know, right? You've got your work cut out for you!

- In some cases you might have to sit Graduate Record Examinations. The GREs are a standardized test that is an admissions requirement for many graduate schools in the United States and Canada. Other countries will have their own equivalents.

  Once you have taken and (hopefully) aced your Graduate Record Examinations, you can then start applying to veterinary schools. Depending on which country you are in, refer to the schools section listed at the back of this book for some prestigious schools to send your application into. Make sure to include everything from your SAT/ACT (GCSE/A-Level) results, GPA, GRE score and the places you have volunteered. Leave nothing out which could potentially increase your chances of getting accepted. More is better when it comes to your application.

- Now you're in vet school — congratulations! Your time here will be even more vigorous and focused than all the studying you have done before. This is the final hurdle — unless you would like to be specialized — before you can be certified as a veterinary doctor. Not to scare you, but if you lack focus and commitment at this point and fail your final exams, all your previous qualifications and experience won't matter at all.

  If you make it this far, don't assume you have made it and becoming a vet is just matter of time. You need to knuckle-down to your studies and take nothing for granted.

What Veterinary Students Are Taught

If you are focused, determined and unwavering in your pursuit to be a veterinarian, then you will, in no time, be sitting with other students training and studying to be a vet. How cool would that be!

But what do you imagine that would be like? If you said equal parts hard work, focus and fun — or anything close to that — then you are right. But, can you think of which actual courses you would have to take and what topics would be covered? Do you know which would be your favorite, which would be a walk in the park for you or particularly challenging and requiring extra study time?

Good thing you have this book in your hands, so you don't have to think for too long. Listed below are the courses you would be expected to take in veterinary school. Think of it as a peek into the future and use it to help you prepare mentally.

- **Parasitology**

  Since parasites cause many of the diseases suffered by animals, it is crucial that those who will be tasked with treating them understand how these organisms behave. Veterinary students will learn the life cycles, taxonomy, reproductive behavior and feeding habits of several common parasites. They will also be taught the ways in which animal hosts may react to the activities of parasites. Veterinarians should be able to diagnose and treat parasitic diseases.

- **The Animal Body**

  This refers to the anatomy of animals. Students of veterinary science are required to learn and write exams on the structure and functions of the animal body. Veterinarians should master their reproductive, digestive and nervous systems. It may seem to you now like it's all too much to take in, but repetition is the key to mastery. Once you have learned the information, actually practicing veterinary science will make sure it stays with you forever.

- **Communication Skills**

  Remember that vets do not just deal with animals, their

clients are the humans who bring them in and pay for the services.

Veterinarians should develop good talking and listening skills to aid them in explaining sometimes difficult concepts to their clients. A vet who is poor at communicating their thoughts might scare animal owners into thinking a problem is worse than it is. People should feel comfortable talking to a vet about their animals and have the confidence to make informed decisions.

These same communication skills also extend to how a vet can soothe animals. They are likely to get nervous when being examined. Since communication goes beyond speech, vets should learn how to make both animals and their owners feel more relaxed.

- **Ethics**

Vets are required to learn a set of principles which guide them in making decisions that are moral. Veterinarians are not only taught the rules, but are made to understand the reasons why they must follow them. The law will not be forgiving to a vet who does anything outside the established ethical boundaries, even though their intentions might have been good. How to administer drugs and vaccines and what nutritional advice to give to animal owners must all be done within the set morals codes of veterinary medicine.

- **Animal Diseases**

As we have learned earlier, veterinarians are the ones

who stand between animals and humans to prevent us from contracting diseases which our immune systems are not prepared for. These diseases are so numerous that I can't begin to list them in this book — there would be no space for anything else!

A single vet may not know all of these diseases, but they should know what to do when presented with the symptoms of them. Vets learn proactive and preventive measures for dealing with transferred illnesses. They are taught about viruses, bacteria, fungi, etc. They know how to prevent, cure and control any number of animal diseases, but also look for signs that human owners have become unwell.

- **Nutrition**

Vets study what kinds of food animals should and shouldn't eat. Certain foods are harmful to animals and vets are trained to identify which ones can cause problems. Feeding a dog, cat and horse the same diet may be beneficial to one animal but would, very likely, be harmful to the others.

Also, there has been recent discussion in the media about which is better for pets: homemade food or processed animal feed. Vets can help their clients understand the full picture on nutrition and make informed decisions on their own.

- **Vaccines**

Vets take a series of courses on the importance and application of vaccines. They learn how they are prepared and which chemicals are contained in them.

Vaccines are usually made from the same bacterium or parasitic organism that causes an animal to feel sick. For this reason, vets must understand how to give them safely and in which exact doses. They learn the different kinds of vaccines that are available and the diseases they should be used for.

This is a delicate aspect of veterinary science and vets are only certified when they can prove a thorough understanding and mastery over this subject.

- **Wildlife Management**

  Wildlife conservation is very much a hot topic. From animals going extinct to careless and cruel hunters, the spread of diseases, migration, global warming and illegal poachers, veterinarians have a crucial role to play. They must understand the importance of wildlife, its relationship with humans and why we must ensure its continued survival on the Earth.

  Vets learn how to work with wildlife conservationists from around the world and how to treat a wild animal without getting hurt. By the end of the course, they know how to communicate useful information to conservationists about how best to help animals in the wild.

  The ecosystem suffers a great deal when animals are killed indiscriminately, or when global warming — which causes desertification — forces animals to migrate or die from starvation. The vet is an essential player in making sure wildlife is protected.

- **Animal Pain**

Animals do not all exhibit the same symptoms of pain. A prey animal acts very differently from a predator when it feels pain. This behavior towards stress and discomfort also varies from species to species. Regardless of the degree of pain experienced by an animal, it would find it difficult to communicate that to its owner or to other humans, who may not be able to decode the signs.

Vets are taught which changes in the behavior of an animal may point to pain or disease. For example, lackluster behavior in usually playful animals may mean they are suffering; well-targeted questions for the owners are used to determine what level of pain animals are experiencing. Other methods include monitoring heart rate and other vital signs for clues as to whether an animal is experiencing pain, and in what region of its body.

Chapter 3

Life as a vet

Maybe you've read books where a character wakes up in another person's body, or you've seen the movie *Big*, where a child enters the body of an adult and has to go to work!

So, can you imagine waking up as a vet? The alarm rings tomorrow morning and you are much older — and also a certified and experienced veterinarian. What do you think a typical day would be like? Take minute to really imagine it.

Below are a few regular features of a veterinarian's day. See if you guessed right.

Emergencies

It could be a case from the night before, after the vet had left for home. Frequently though, it's cases that are rushed in as the vet resumes for the day. The ethics of veterinary medicine and the conscience of the vet prevents them from refusing to treat the patient. The emergency could be anything from simple stitching to major surgery. Vets are trained to be ready to take on these surprises when they occur.

Can you place yourself in this position? You just got out of your car and stepped into the clinic. You greet your receptionist and the other staff — including technicians and assistants. You have barely sat down in your office when an assistant comes in with the case of a dog that has swallowed a foreign object and needs to be operated on to get it out. There are no other vets on standby to take your place, and as such, you have to get yourself ready to go to the operating room.

Days like this are usually as trying as they are gratifying. Regardless of how sudden these situations might arise, vets are expected to give their best every time. You need to prioritize your workload and deal with the critical cases first.

Examinations

Another part of the day is examining animals for various diseases. Sometimes they are routine, and other times they are emergencies. Vets take the symptoms of an illness and go further to look for less obvious signs to confirm a diagnosis.

Besides surgery, this is usually the most common part of a veterinarian's day. Some examinations are booked days in advance, others are booked on the day. A vet will carry out as many as ten examinations in a single day. Each one requires focus and deduction so the vet can come to as precise a diagnosis as possible.

Can you place yourself in this position? You just spent close to 30 minutes asking a cat's owner in-depth questions about the history of their pet's health and the symptoms it has now been exhibiting. As accurate as they are with the answers, you still have to thoroughly examine the cat physically.

After 10 minutes you believe you have arrived at a conclusive diagnosis. You disclose this to the cat's owner, and they become upset as they now have to make a difficult decision about whether to opt for surgery, which is not only risky but expensive. They leave to consider the decision.

But there's no time for you to sit back and relax. A hamster is waiting to be examined. You can't keep them waiting. There are also a few more animals on the list for today. Some you will treat today, others will have to wait until the next day. While the job of a vet is rewarding, it can also be hectic and challenging.

Getting Scratched

Every job has its hazards. The barrier of communication between human and animal still poses a problem when vets try to examine or treat animals.

Cats are especially prone to jumping on vets during treatments. They might be relaxed at first, but when they have more of an idea of what is to come, they can become very distressed very quickly. Getting scratched is also not the only way vets can get hurt by the animals they treat. Horses, dogs, goats and other animals find ways to express their displeasure in a manner which often puts the vet in harm's way.

Can you place yourself in this position? You are already tired from all the consulting, surgeries and examining you've done today. Yet, one last cat will need a vaccination.

Imagine that you are still relatively new to the practice and, as a result, prone to making some of the rookie mistakes of veterinary medicine. You inject the cat with the vaccine, but the cat is startled and scratches you close to your eye. It's not so deep, but it's bleeding nonetheless. Now you've got to treat yourself also for a possible infection. But at least the cat has had his vaccine!

Surgery

Surgeries, like examinations, may be booked in advance or be emergency cases that need to be done on the day. An operation may be more energy-intensive than you think. They require precise hand-eye coordination and lots of focus and concentration. The lives of animals hang in the balance during these procedures, and there might be the risk of disabling the animal if you are not careful and precise.

As a result of these factors, surgical procedures are never a walk in the park. The satisfaction comes after the operation is a success and the vet's clients (both human and animal) are well and happy.

Enemas

Have you heard stories of people or animals having one? They are, to put it mildly, slightly unpleasant. A vet trying to give a dog (or any other animal for that matter) an enema is likely to be sprayed with poop. I know that sounds disgusting but vets, generally, do not mind this part of the job. The fact is, you need to become accustomed to these kinds of tasks and see them as a part of the range of duties that come with being a vet.

As dirty and as fear-inducing as it might seem to you now, this is a key part of veterinary medicine for many animal doctors. This is because animals usually feel a lot better after they've had an enema. Issues of constipation and other forms of discomfort are reduced. What may seem like a tough task for you is going to vastly improve the life of an animal.

As a vet, your assistant or the animal owner would have to hold your patient in place while you perform the enema. Poop on your coat and scratches on your arm might be the price you have to pay for carrying out the procedure.

More emergencies, examinations and surgeries

If you thought that a vet's day ended with just a few of the activities listed above, then you are mistaken. A regular day in a vet's life can, very often, begin by 8am and end at 5pm-6pm. There would be more animals to examine, more emergencies to handle and, probably, more surgeries to conduct. People keep bringing in their animals, even at odd hours of the day. Whatever a vet can't handle in one day is bumped over to the next.

Can you place yourself in this position? Right after veterinary school, when you begin your practice, you may believe things will get easier from that point on. While in school, you had to study incredibly hard and try your best to make good grades. The real world can turn out to be more demanding. There will be ongoing studying and later hours. On the upside, there will be no more exams. But, they will be replaced by real-life tests of your skills. However, if you are committed to the vocation, the satisfaction of bringing relief and health to animals will make all your effort seem worthwhile.

Chapter 4

Is Veterinary Medicine the Right Career for You?

Veterinary medicine is a demanding career that asks a lot of you and takes dedication and sacrifice. However, if it is your dream to be a vet than you won't feel satisfied doing anything else as a career. To help you decide if it really is the right career for you, here's a list of qualities that good vets possess. Read through this list and ask yourself, is this the kind of person I am? If so, you'll make a great vet!

You love helping animals

This is, first and foremost, the most critical deciding factor when it comes to the veterinary profession. There isn't much that can be said if a person has always found it boring or annoying to take care of animals. Not every one of us will like the same things. But when it comes to veterinary medicine, an affinity for animals is an absolute must.

Maybe you only love dogs or horses or certain species of birds. What is important is that you like at least one category — remember, as vet you can always specialize. And not only should you like them, but you should also want to help them and learn about them.

Veterinarians have to treat many animals in a day — sometimes as many as fifteen or twenty. Their owners bring in these animals with diverse medical issues. To excel in this practice, it requires an individual who doesn't mind sacrificing time and energy to make sure that animals feel better. Some tasks may be rather unpleasant, so you need a great deal of affection for animals to get you through the process of curing or managing their illnesses.

This is one reasons why it is usually vital that you volunteer at clinics — to get a feel for the job. You'll get to see vets in action, saving animals and performing a variety of activities. It doesn't matter in what capacity you volunteer, even if it is just cleaning the cages. You will still get a feel for the working environment and determine if veterinary medicine is a good fit for you.

You are a patient person

This could easily be deduced from what we have covered in the book so far. Patience is a crucial quality for every vet. Whatever it is that an animal feels, the difficulty in conveying this information poses problems between animals and vets. Animals may be jerky or flighty simply out of fear. It would be your job to make these animals comfortable, so you can administer whatever treatment is required.

But since animals do not bring themselves to a vet's clinic, you would also have to be patient with the humans who bring them in. Some owners are more attached to their pets than they are to the humans in their lives. Many see their animals as valid members of their families, just like children. This kind of bond between human and animal may cause the owners of these pets to behave irrationally at times. They might blow things out of proportion, raise their voices, speak rudely and opt for bad decisions.

Your temper, throughout all of these interactions, must remain even and calm. You should be able to talk to animal owners in a tone that is not patronizing or too technical. In this way, you will help them to make decisions that are best for their animals.

You love science stuff

You probably know by now that students are least likely to be successful in subjects they dislike. Most of your education as a trainee vet will be science-based. If you haven't enjoyed science classes up until this point, it could pose a big problem.

Doing well in subjects such as mathematics and biology will be central to you getting accepted into university to study veterinary science. Having top grades in these subjects will boost your chances of being selected by the most prestigious veterinary schools. You will need an appreciation for all things science related to make sure you stay interested in the course and up-to-date with new research throughout your career and practice in the field.

This is why you should never be forced or manipulated into choosing to become a veterinarian. Some may study to become a vet for reasons besides a love for animals and interest in doing it. These reasons may include the financial rewards or social status that come with being a vet. Such students attend lectures and cram texts to pass their exams.

However, after a few years of practicing, they start feeling underwhelmed, unfulfilled and bored. They think that, since there are no more exams they must study for, they do not need to keep reading on topics related to their field of practice. Unlike other vets who are genuinely excited by their jobs, they do not enjoy trying out new procedures or technology. Soon they get left behind as the field moves forward and they realize they no longer have the skills to remain competitive or relevant.

Vets like this do not give their best to the animals who are brought to them for help. Veterinary medicine is, in every way, a scientific profession that is always changing and advancing. Make sure you are happy with science as a core subject before jumping in.

You like to keep learning

A hallmark of good vets is that they keep bettering their knowledge and skills. They are always reading to update their knowledge and attending workshops and seminars to improve their skills. Vets who are passionate about their jobs may even try to come up with new medical inventions or procedures.

New and improved ways to treat illness, injuries and correct defects are introduced to the world of veterinary medicine every year. Choosing to keep abreast of these changes will mean the difference between offering a cutting-edge modern service and stagnating or using out-dated techniques.

By extension, it will also determine how many clients walk through the doors of your clinic every day. People may cultivate strong relationships with their vets, but what matters most to them are results. They want to see their animals regain their full health in the shortest time possible, and they will want a vet who can provide a modern, efficient service.

Unless you want to end up as the vet who is always making excuses and is way behind on the best ways of treating animals, you've got to love learning. Do you? If your answer to this is yes, then a doctorate in veterinary medicine might be your calling.

You pay attention to details

How meticulous are you? Big word, right? Meticulous is simply a way to describe how detailed a person is. In other words, this is the precision with which they handle any project. Some other words for meticulous are detailed and careful.

Let's get down to how meticulousness is important to a vet. Two words can explain the reason for this correctly: medicine and surgery.

Every aspect of medicine demands caution and precision. Vets and doctors must be accurate in their diagnoses, administration of drugs, vaccines and other forms of intravenous (meaning: inside the body and related to veins) medications, and in the advice offered to animal owners.

But surgery is a particularly painstaking and challenging branch of medicine. Vets must be extra careful, without getting lost in their worries or fears of making an error. If you are naturally someone who is meticulous, thorough and detailed about aspects of life, then you'll do fine as a vet.

You are not too squeamish

I probably don't have to say too much here. I'm sure you know that a regular day in a vet's life usually features things like blood and vomit. They are part and parcel of the treatment of animals.

During working hours, vets have to deal with issues and stresses not faced by many other professions. It is the joy they bring to animal owners and the relief felt by the animals when they return to health which makes it all worth it for the veterinarian.

Not being squeamish doesn't only refer to having the stomach for the sight of blood. People can be squeamish when faced with tough decisions, such as whether to put an animal down or not. Vets have got to keep a level head and be a shoulder for their clients to cry on when they need it. They do not shy away from proposing tough solutions, regardless of how risky or distressing they might be. Emotional strength and empathy are key requirements for vets.

You believe in hard work

Finally, the most important principle for success in any job is probably hard work. This is not to say that hard work is a guarantee for success, but instead that fortune does not smile on the lazy.

Vets who stay at home three days a week cannot hope to pay off their student loans in a few years. They will always be cutting it close with their mortgage and other payments. There will be little opportunity for them to save up enough money to buy some of the things they would like in life. There is also the problem of a lazy vet's clients leaving them for a more diligent one.

People need answers, advice and treatment for their animals, and new cases come in everyday. You've got to be available more often than not to keep the majority of your clients happy. This job requires a great deal of face time.

How hardworking are you with your schoolwork? How about with helping around the house? If you aren't very hardworking now, no need to fret. This is one virtue that you can start developing until it becomes a habit. Start working hard and turn it into your default setting.

Summary

Which of the above qualities do you possess now, and which do you feel you should work on? I don't expect you to have every one of them but, if you still want to be a vet, you now know some of the key qualities that are required.

Make sure your goal of being a vet is something that you want to do and is not an endeavor that is being forced on you. If your mom and dad insist you must be a vet, despite you not being sure, then talk to them about it and express your feelings. Don't embark on the profession for the money or status alone. Make sure you love animals and are prepared to learn new things throughout your career.

If it is your decision to be a vet because you are excited and passionate about it, then go for it with all you have. It will be the best decision that you ever made.

Chapter 5

The Hardest Parts of Being a Vet

This chapter of the book is not designed to scare or dissuade you from your dream of becoming a vet. Balanced information means that both sides of every subject must be presented. This is why an entire chapter has been devoted to the potential not-so-pleasant side of veterinary medicine. Don't worry, I'll talk about the attractive side in the next chapter!

Even though the aspects of the job that will be listed in this chapter may not be appealing to some, they could be rewarding and interesting to you. It all depends on which perspective you are looking at it from and how you react to challenging situations.

Vets have to carry out a number of varied tasks on a daily

basis. If you truly have a passion for the job — if you love animals and will go out of your way to make them well — you will happily accept these challenges.

Don't be deceived into thinking there is a job out there with only benefits and no drawbacks (well, maybe an ice-cream taster!). The fact is, every job will have parts that you will find either dull, repetitive of even unpleasant. There will be days when you will feel like quitting. You'll go home tired and it may seem, for a moment, to not be worth the stress.

It is during such times that you have to remind yourself of your reasons for choosing to be a vet. This is why the motivation of becoming rich and getting recognition is not good enough to build a career on. They are not solid and reliable enough to fall back on when the going gets tough. However, being a vet is not like doing a standard office job.

This is why veterinarians are heroes. When you combine medicine and animals, you have one of the most demanding jobs out there. Still, vets keep going. They know that, without them, animals in distress around the world have very little chance at a good quality of life. For this reason, they never back down. They share the joy of both their human and animal clients, and this is all they need to be satisfied with their job. The rewards make all the difficult tasks more than worthwhile.

Now let's look at some of the tough parts of the job.

Euthanasia

Sometimes, either as a result of aging or an incurable illness, the only option is to end an animal's life in a way that is painless. After a quick injection, the client can hold their animal as it takes their last breath.

You may not think that vets feel any sadness during this procedure, but the majority of them do. They see animals come in regularly with a variety of issues. Often, they form strong bonds with them. So, it is also hard on the vet when that animal has, for whatever reason, come to the end of its life.

It's also hard when vets have to advise clients to take this decision. Some vets are comfortable expressing their emotions during these occasions, but others would rather remain strong for their clients. They want the animal owners to know that euthanasia, regardless of how drastic an action it seems, is the only humane option at this point — much better than allowing the animal to suffer in pain and discomfort. Sometimes there is relief is seeing suffering come to an end.

Euthanasia is a common aspect of veterinary medicine and, depending on the situation, may be truly saddening.

Bad animal owners

Vets have to deal with all sorts of animal owners, even those who show little signs of care towards their animals. This kind of client may go as far as requesting euthanasia for their animals simply to get rid of them.

As has been mentioned earlier in this book, veterinarians are usually individuals who are passionate about helping animals. They love animals and are willing to go the extra mile to allow them to live quality and healthy lives. You can imagine how difficult it would be for them to watch clients who are indifferent towards the suffering of their animals and would rather not be bothered.

Then, there is a different group of animal owners. These

actually care about their animals, but are so ignorant of the right way to treat them that they inadvertently end up hurting them.

It is not an easy thing for a vet to watch this happen, especially when the clients are set in their ways. Some animal owners are convinced that their way of caring for their animals is right and could not possibly be the cause of their problems. Sometimes, these kinds of clients will only accept fault after their animals have paid the price for their ignorance and unwillingness to change.

Money issues

Discussing money when the life of an animal is on the line is never easy for a vet. So it is often difficult to address the issue with clients. Some clinics do not offer treatment unless a down-payment has been made in advance. Certain clients are offended by this practice and see the vet as greedy or immoral.

Knowing all you do about vets, I doubt you will come to the same conclusion. Vets love animals, often even more than the clients themselves. If they could, they would offer to treat animals without requesting payment. But that is largely impossible.

The cost of running a successful clinic, which includes paying staff and bills which keep the hospital functioning, comes from the payments made by clients when a service has been given to them. Also — and this is especially true of newer vets — veterinarians have to pay off large student loans, which can run into tens of thousands of dollars.

There are clients who are not very forthcoming about their financial situation. Stories abound of clients who promise to pay after surgery or any other treatment has been performed. In the end, these clients don't follow through with their promises and the vet suffers the loss. This discourages the veterinarian from offering services in the future on the basis of a promise of payment. Veterinary clinics are not charities. They need to make money in order to survive and thrive.

Sometimes clients are unable to pay, but their pets are suffering. In these instances the clinic has to decide whether to discount the price of treatment or turn away the client. These are very difficult decision for all concerned.

Giving bad news

No one, in their right minds anyway, has a pleasant time doing this. It's sad having to deliver information you know will break the other person's heart and ruin their day.

You may have found yourself having to do the same thing in the past. Say you were playing in the house and broke a favorite object of your father's. Knowing he would find out either way, you choose to tell the truth even though it might hurt him and make him mad at you. Can you recall the fear and trepidation you felt in breaking the news and waiting for the unpredictable reaction from the other person?

Sometimes, an animal may have come to the end of its life, either due to old age or disease. Other times, it is a serious issue such as permanent blindness or amputation, which a vet would have to discuss with their client.

Animal owners may, at this point, become very emotional and their behavior could become unpredictable. They might accuse the doctor of not doing enough, not having the right qualifications or just being incompetent. Clients may cry, plead, get mad, curse or storm out with their animals. You can see why a vet has to be sensitive, empathetic and careful in delivering bad news to their clients.

Chapter 6

The Best Parts of Being a Vet

Now that I have said a little about the downsides of veterinary practice, which hopefully has not shaken your resolve to continue with your dream of being a vet, I must share the many upsides.

It is only fitting that I share with you the things which keep vets going every day. Despite the hassle and stress of the job, there are many things that veterinarians look forward to and love about the role.

I have listed them for you. Some vets might have more reasons on their list; some, more personal than others. Use this as a guide and let it help you in standing firm on your goal of becoming a veterinarian.

Passion

Since you already have hopes of becoming a vet, I can deduce that this feeling will grow into one of passion as the years roll by. This book, I'm sure, has already done a great deal in giving you a more rounded and lifelike view of veterinary medicine.

As you get older, you will probably find newer and much deeper reasons why you have chosen veterinary medicine out of every other rewarding profession available. Regardless, then, of the obstacles you might face in your pursuit of bringing aid to animals, you will have this passion to keep you focused and happy.

This happiness, which many vets go home from work with, is the most important part of it all. Not everyone gets to work in a job that they are truly excited about. The motivation for many people, and this is mostly justifiable, is money. Their driving force is a desire to be wealthy or to pay the bills, but this may not hold up for very long. In moments of deep introspection, when every achievement and decision in a person's life is questioned, money is not likely to stand as a convincing motivator.

Passion, on the other hand, makes all the effort count. Making money from a job that makes your soul joyful, keeps your mind engaged and fills your heart with excitement is the happiest combination of all.

Adding value to animals

In contrast to many jobs today, veterinary medicine gives rather than takes. Many of us live in societies that are driven by personal gain. As such, it is truly honorable to break from this mold and serve, instead of looking to be served.

Veterinarians are happy to do just this, and for animals, too. They sacrifice the better part of their day and energy towards bringing good health to animals. They strengthen the ties between humans and their pets. This they do, not just by treating the animals, but also as a result of the advice they give to animal owners.

Adding value to humans

This brings us to the next point. After sitting with a vet for a few minutes, people often leave enlightened. Clients gain clarity, and this makes them less impatient, angry or confused towards their animals. They now understand why an animal behaves in the way it does, and how they can control or work around it.

As a result of the efforts of veterinarians, there are fewer cases of people getting disillusioned with owning pets or animals dying because of the ignorance of their owners. What better job is there than one which meets the needs of both humans and animals and brings them closer together?

Salary

How could I end this list without talking about good-old money?

It is true, like I have pointed out repeatedly, that many vets do not get into the profession as a means of becoming rich. It is usually a matter of passion, but the money truly doesn't hurt. Veterinarians make as much as $100,000 every year. This, I might add, would be more than enough to pay off your student debts and still live a comfortable life —with some luxury too, if you're into that.

Although, keep in mind, that the salary of vets differs from country to country and according to where a vet chooses to work; some veterinarians start up private practices and others choose to work for the government.

Regardless of these factors, a vet's wages in a year is unlikely to fall below $60,000. You'll have to find a good neighborhood where there is a high demand for animal doctors (you could choose places with ranches or communities with a large number of pet owners), and work really hard.

This is what usually separates successful vets from their less successful counterparts. When you become a vet, make it a duty to be available most of the time. Be friendly with both humans and animals and offer as affordable a price as you can manage. In no time at all, your clinic will have grown in popularity and, as a consequence of this, in financial strength too. It all comes down to hard work and building trust.

Chapter 7

What You Can Start Doing Now

There are some excellent ways in which you can start preparing to become a vet. Not only will it act as an added boost to your application to veterinary school, but it will also enlighten you concerning veterinary medicine.

Joining veterinary clubs, going on camping trips and volunteering are a few options. Listed and explained below is what you can start doing now. Hoping and wishing alone does not bring dreams into reality. You must play an active part if you want to have a good chance of living your dream.

Working towards your goal now, as young as you are, is the best time to begin.

Your applications to university and veterinary school will contain these various activities, which validate your passion for the profession. You will have hands-on knowledge, which ensures you stand out from the crowd.

This knowledge will also place you miles ahead of your peers. Very little will be able to sway you from your dream or shake your resolve. This is how to be the very best at anything. It isn't just about how you can memorize information for tests. It is more about how involved you are; mind, body and heart.

Let's look at this list of fun and enlightening activities.

Read Books

Books such as this one, *How to Become a Veterinarian,* are great tools for preparing you for all that veterinary medicine entails.

So, I should congratulate you then for already making one right move towards your dream. Well done. Just think of how far ahead of your peers you are. You know things they don't. As much as you admire veterinary medicine, you are also aware of what others might call downsides. You know how you could handle them without feeling discouraged. You know the steps that will help you to become a vet, and you know what happens after.

After reading any book about veterinary medicine, ask yourself a few questions. Take this book, for example. Ask yourself what you have learned up to this point. How will you use the information you have taken in to steer yourself towards achieving your dream? Questions like these are actionable. They ensure you don't stay still, even after learning new things.

When you are done reading this book, feel free to visit a nearby library or bookstore to find more books. Use Google to search for similar books, and fill your mind with useful information.

There are also more technical books available on the subject, if you would like to read those. Don't feel daunted by the size of those kinds of books, or the advanced grammar used in them. Whether the book is on anatomy or animal diseases, the more you read them without distraction, the more you'll find them easier to understand.

Join Veterinary Groups/Clubs/Camps

There are certain groups for animal enthusiasts that are available to children of various ages. They give kids the opportunity to experience catering for animals outside of books and TV shows. You will also meet other children like yourself, who love helping animals, too.

These veterinary groups and clubs have become very popular as a result of the combination of fun and education. What better way is there to convince both children and their parents of a career path? The kids want an adventure, but their parents would like them to learn useful skills that will aid them in becoming valuable members of society when they grow up.

Veterinary clubs are a good place to experience both. The kids are given exciting activities which enhance their knowledge and teach them about animal behaviors.

Camps are also an excellent way to get yourself used to animal care. Instead of being a member of a club, you could have the same experience — but only for a day. You'll play with animals, clean up after them and learn some basic medical treatments for them.

Here are some popular veterinary clubs and camps you can join.

1. Cub Creek Science Camp

2. Future Vet Kids Camp

3. Avian Adventure Summer Camp

4. Canine Good Manners Camp

5. Animal Kingdom Camp

6. Kids Vet Club

7. Pets 'n' Vets (Junior Vet Club)

8. Royal Veterinary College (Junior Vet Club)

Watch Documentaries

Documentaries about animals that are shown on TV or made available on the internet have been the reason why many people have chosen to become vets. Besides the entertainment which the whole family can enjoy, they reveal a variety of problems to be solved by vets.

Among these are animal diseases which may be spreading. Leaving this to continue would not only spell the extinction of certain animals, but would affect the human population also. There are tribes living close to these animals, who hunt them for food. Veterinarians are in the frontline in the battle against pandemics.

Documentaries also explain things such as global warming,

which leads to desertification and volatile weather conditions. These force animals to migrate in search of food and water. Survival of the species is the first and foremost instinct of every living creature. Veterinarians have a role to play in the conservation of wildlife.

Sometimes, these documentaries may deviate from the usual wildlife exposé and venture into pets and livestock. They educate viewers about first aid methods for treating animals and which nutrients are best for certain animals. By watching documentaries, you will learn why animals behave the way they do and just how they fit into our lives.

Ask Questions

There is a wise saying which goes: those who ask questions will never get lost along the way. In your journey to becoming a vet, there will be so many things that you do not know — and no one expects you to. But personal development means that you need to work on increasing your knowledge of various topics.

This you can achieve in any number of ways. By reading books, surfing the internet, watching programs on television and attending classes. But there is an even faster and more direct way to accomplish this. You simply have to ask the right people the right questions.

These questions may be directed at your parents, teachers or a local vet. Make sure you seek answers to every question which nags at you. You will find that people are usually only too happy to help you. If anyone is impatient and refuses to answer, do not let that discourage you. Maybe that person is having a bad day or they dislike answering questions. Ask someone else.

Volunteer at Clinics

As you grow older, you may want an even better example of a veterinarian in action. Everything that has been said about vets in this book, you can see for yourself. Watch vets bring healing and joy to animals and their human owners, and observe how both stressful and fulfilling it is. Assist them in whatever way you can to share in that fulfillment.

You can even learn a few things from the veterinary technicians. For example, how do they take fluid samples from animals? How do they test those fluid samples? What procedures go into preparing an animal for surgery? These and many more important things are what you can learn from volunteering.

While at the clinic, take notes if you must. We all don't share the same personality type, but make an effort to get close to the medical staff of the clinic, even if you may be an introvert. Ask questions, take pictures if you are allowed to and, generally, make sure your time at the clinic is spent productively.

Keep in mind, if you are able to find this opportunity, volunteering at a veterinary clinic will be extra rewarding because university boards and veterinary schools will rate your application very highly. At your interview you've got to have an interesting story to tell about your time there. There has to be a list of things you learned, and you need to explain how your experience has confirmed your choice to be a vet.

Get a Pet

In your pursuit of a career in the field of veterinary medicine, owning and caring for a pet is one of the very best ways to get an appreciation for the animal kingdom. Sharing a living space with an animal will develop your patience and foster appreciation, which cannot be taught by even the most respected universities in the world. You will bathe your pet, feed it, clean its poop and be there for it whenever it falls ill.

So many of the things you'll learn in vet school will already have come to you naturally. Who better to teach humans how to take care of animals than the animals themselves? You only have to be attentive and alert.

By observing the patterns of your pet's behavior, you will have prepared your mind for a life in veterinary medicine. Many of the things that other individuals will have to get accustomed to will already be a part of your daily life. Owning a pet teaches you to be responsible and patient.

Instead of a regular domestic pet, you might prefer a pony, pig or hen. The objective would still be to ensure that these animals are healthy and happy. You should talk to your parents about getting you an animal, which is affordable for them and manageable for you. Tell them it will be a great help towards preparing you for life as a vet. Good luck!

Visit the Zoo

I'm sure you've got a zoo in your local area. If not, then it shouldn't be too far from you. Even if it is, try convincing your parents to take you to visit one. It doesn't have to be often, just once a year would do fine.

This is the closest you may be able to get to wild and exotic animals, besides watching them on television. Why is this important? It is because wild and domesticated animals do not behave in the same ways. Their reactions to humans, nutritional needs and social structures vary widely. And who knows, maybe after seeing one for real, you just might want to specialize as a wildlife or exotic animal doctor.

It is alright if you have become attached to your cat, dog or horse and would rather care for milder animals. Also, you are not the only one afraid of untamed animals!

What you should understand is that wild animals need our help, too. They often go through difficult and painful labor during childbirth. Like your dog, they might swallow foreign materials which are not digestible and require surgery to get them out. They get injured during fights, playtime or by a variety of other means. They can feel weak, feverish, constipated or nauseated.

Vets need to understand how to help them without risking their own lives. Watching them in these "man-made" natural habitats might give you an appreciation for these animals and a sense of how to behave around them.

Take Science Classes

You're going to have to attend a bunch of them as you go further with your veterinary education, so you might as well develop a liking for them now. Your friends might shy away from these subjects and call them unnecessarily difficult, but you don't have this luxury.

Subjects such as biology, mathematics and chemistry have to be your cup of tea. This does not to mean that science is more important than every other field of study. It only means that certain subjects, like the ones I have listed, are prerequisites to every course you will take in university and in veterinary school.

But there is good news. The more time you spend with any subject, mathematics for example, the easier it becomes for you. Your brain is flexible enough to adjust to the pattern of reasoning required by the subject.

You only have to be consistent, focused and intentional with your study time. Even better news, you do not have to give up the other classes you enjoy. Being a vet doesn't exclude you from other activities. Say you love poetry, for example. By all means, you can be a vet and a poet. You could take poetry as an elective in university.

This means you have to learn to manage your time productively, though.

Have Like-minded Friends

Hanging out with the right friends will not only keep your goal in focus, but you will also be motivated by peers who share your mindset. Having conversations with your friends about animals will commit certain facts and terms that are related to veterinary medicine to your memory. If you keep the company of people who share similar dreams with you, you'll be influenced to do the things which will prove helpful to you in the future.

You may have heard this cliché from your parents: evil communication corrupts good manners. As overused as that statement is, it is an accurate psychological fact. No matter how independent you believe your opinions to be, they are still largely influenced by your family, the community you live in and your friends. This means that to grow and expand your horizons you need to find like-minded people.

Chapter 8

Veterinary Assistants

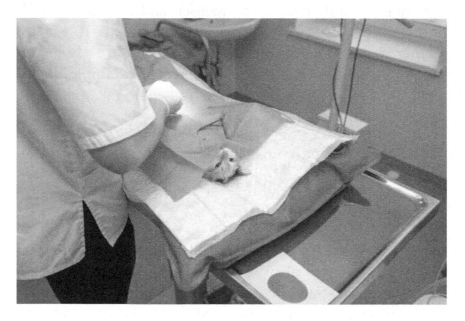

Vets aren't the only ones working closely with animals in a clinic. The role of veterinary assistant and veterinary technician are crucial to the process of helping animals get better. They perform a range of important tasks that help the vets in their daily work. They can even sometimes stand in for the vet to perform certain treatments on animals. They are also responsible for the animals' after-care and dealing with the owners. Let's look at these critical roles more closely.

What is a Veterinary Assistant?

Just from the name, you might get an idea of the job and duties of a veterinary assistant. A veterinary assistant is a person who works under a vet or veterinary technician in the position of a general helper. This person carries out different tasks according to instructions, and under the supervision of a veterinarian or vet technician.

The tasks a veterinary assistant does involves being responsible for the animals in relation to the discipline of the vet (farm, pets, exotic, etc.). They are meant to see to the basic needs of the animal patients and offer general care such as exercising, bathing and feeding the animals.

The veterinary assistant is also meant to keep the animals calm and under control when they are being examined by the veterinarian.

Simply put, veterinary assistants see to the welfare of animals in clinics, laboratories, research centers and animal hospitals.

Also, it is the job of the veterinary assistant to care for veterinary equipment and laboratories. They make sure that laboratory equipment, examination tables and operating rooms are kept sterilized, clean and organized.

Owing to their role as assistants to vets, veterinary assistants can be classified as "paraveterinary" workers. This makes them able to perform other veterinary duties such as collecting samples of blood, urine, fur etc. They can also administer treatments to animals in the form of vaccines or medicines.

However, they are only allowed to perform these duties in regards to laboratory work according to their certification and the laws in their region. Also, they can fill in as clerks or secretaries to the veterinarian and help organize their schedule, receive patients and give mini-lectures to animal owners, as well as seeing to their concerns and questions.

Veterinary assistants are important to the field of veterinary medicine because they effectively manage the relationship between vets, animals and animal owners. They form the middle part which links all three parties together and ensures satisfaction for the client.

How to Become a Veterinary Assistant

The job requirements of a veterinary assistant vary from one location to another. In some areas, little to no formal certification in animal biology and health is required for the job. In these places, the veterinary assistant is trained to meet the standards of the vet in order to help the clinic operate efficiently.

The training program is usually conducted by the veterinarian or a special training team in the place of work. Even after completing the training, the veterinary assistant is still expected to depend on the vet for instructions, further training and guidance while working for him or her.

Since no legally binding certifications or licenses are used in obtaining the role of a veterinary assistant in these places, the assistant is limited to performing certain duties which the laws of the region allow.

These laws may limit the work done by the assistant in regards to direct contact with animals, like giving medications and withdrawing samples of blood and saliva for laboratory purposes. This is because these duties require certification and are left to higher qualified and registered veterinary personnel such as veterinarians, veterinary technicians or veterinary nurses.

In other locations, a person applying for the job of a veterinary assistant would be required to have a certain level of legal certification, a license or experience. In these areas, veterinary organizations are more likely to employ persons with previous experience in animal care, educational qualifications or those who hold a practice license.

The educational qualifications in these areas could be a high school diploma or a major in any animal-related course. Even with these qualifications, the assistant would still be trained by the organization to meet their standards and requirements.

To be better equipped for this role, one might want to apply to a veterinary body such as NAVTA — National Association of Veterinary Technicians in America — to be certified as an AVA — Approved Veterinary Assistant. To become an AVA, the applicant takes the approved training programs and examinations organized by the veterinary body.

When the program is successfully completed, the applicant is given a certificate that qualifies them to apply for the role of a veterinary assistant.

What Are the Key Duties of a Veterinary Assistant?

As a veterinary assistant, you are expected to perform many specific tasks carefully and without error. These tasks could be clerical activities, laboratory work and animal-related work among other things.

Some of the duties of veterinary assistants are listed below.

1. They see to the wellbeing of the animals in their care, providing these animals with their basic daily needs. These could be exercising, bathing, feeding, cleaning their cages, etc.

2. Veterinary assistants are in charge of making sure the areas, equipment and tools used in the treatment of animals are clean, sterilized and stored tidily.

3. Veterinary assistants are expected to help in laboratory proceedings like withdrawing samples of saliva, urine, tissue and blood from animals.

4. It is the duty of veterinary assistants to clean up the resting areas of animal patients, disinfect them of germs and clean up their treatment rooms after each session.

5. In the case of an emergency, veterinary assistants can provide first-aid treatment to an injured or sick animal before the arrival of a vet.

6. It is the duty of veterinary assistants to give immunizations and medications to animals according to the instructions of the vet.

7. Veterinary assistants help answer the questions of animal owners, talk to them about how to better care for their animals, receive their concerns over their animals and relieve their fears.

8. Veterinary assistants help keep animals under control during veterinary procedures such as sample withdrawal, medication dosing and surgery.

9. Veterinary assistants are expected to manage the medical charts, noting any changes in animals as they are cared for daily.

10. It is their job to carry out simple laboratory work like the examination of feces, taking an ultrasound, giving x-rays, analyzing animal urine and recording their vital signs.

11. Veterinary assistants are the ones who receive new patients for the veterinarian and enter their details into the clinic's records.

12. They run daily checks on the animals to know the state of their health and help protect them against sicknesses such as Feline immunodeficiency virus, heartworm and lice.

13. Before and after every surgical procedure on an animal, it is the veterinary assistants who care for it. They also observe and report on the health of the animal after the surgery to the vet.

14. Veterinary assistants act as a bridge of information between the veterinarian, the animal and its owner. They supply the animal owner with information from the vet such as prescriptions, diet and care details.

15. It is the job of veterinary assistants to make an animal feel at ease in its new surroundings and undergo its treatment smoothly.

16. In the case of an abused animal or an animal in its final stage of life, veterinary assistants provide moral support for the owners.

17. They also help in putting down animals that can't be treated or cared for.

18. It is the job of veterinary assistants to make first contact with clients, receive and introduce them to the vet.

What Qualities and Skills Are Needed by Veterinary Assistants?

To be successful in the role of a veterinary assistant, you must have skills and qualities that are important to animal care and human relations. These skills and qualities could be personal or the technical ones acquired during training.

Some of these are listed below.

Good Listening Skills

To be a successful veterinary assistant, you must have good listening skills so you are able to receive, record and follow the instructions of the vet or veterinary technician. Also, this skill helps you to better understand the concerns and questions of animal owners for easy documentation and communication with the vet.

Love and Passion for Animals

A person can only be successful in this role if they love animals and are passionate about caring for them. This quality is necessary because, sometimes, the job can be tough and hectic. You need a good reason why you want to do the role of veterinary assistant.

Good Observational Skills

Since it is the job of a veterinary assistant to monitor and care for animals before and after surgical procedures, they have to have good observation skills. This is because veterinary assistants need to be able to note changes in the conditions of the animals and report back to the vet, who can then take a suitable course of action.

Agility and Physical Fitness

The job of a veterinary assistant can be really demanding; as such, if you have little or no physical stamina then you can be easily worn out. This is why anyone applying for the role must be in good shape physically so they are able to keep animals under control, or move or lift them as the case may be. A good level of fitness would also help them withstand a long, challenging workday without feeling too tired to help the vet. Also, a veterinary assistant needs to be agile in order to carry out a number of duties quickly and efficiently.

Work Oriented

The role of a veterinary assistant revolves around being helpful to others, so those applying for the role must have the desire to help. They must also be diligent and thorough when it comes to supporting the veterinarian, the veterinary technician, the animals themselves and animal owners.

Speed and Multitasking

Anyone applying for the role of a veterinary assistant should be quick-witted and capable of doing more than one task at a time. This helps ease any friction that might occur, reduces workload and quickens veterinary procedures.

Focus

Without good focus, a veterinary assistant cannot function in the manner they need to. A veterinary assistant is expected to pay attention to small details during any animal checks and provide accurate reports to the vet.

Temperament and Crisis Management

Since the job involves interacting with animal owners, animals themselves and more senior veterinary personnel, the veterinary assistant is expected to manage the relationship between these three parties smoothly. Since the major part involves human interaction, veterinary assistants are expected to watch their tempers and help keep other parties calm and collected. It is further expected of veterinary assistants to show emotional care when communicating with owners of animals that are very ill or ready to be put down.

Ability to Solve Problems

Veterinary assistants should be able to prevent troubles from breaking out in the workplace. Should problems arise, they are expected to solve them quickly and thoroughly to prevent further issues.

Stress Management

To perform effectively in the role of a veterinary assistant, they are expected to show calmness and go about their duties patiently. This is because the visiting animals and their owners all have different personalities and might react unfavorably if approached in a certain manner. Should an animal be aggressive or unwilling, a veterinary assistant is meant to handle it patiently without losing their wits. They must, therefore, be able to keep calm when faced with a difficult animal patient but still be firm enough to ensure that it settles and is put under control.

Fun Facts about Veterinary Assistants

- They get to be around animals every day, sometimes even more than vets themselves.

- They have fun with animals by exercising, feeding and cleaning them.

- They get to learn new things daily about animals and how to care for them.

- They become better animal owners.

- They get the chance to teach others about caring for animals.

Chapter 9

Veterinary Technicians

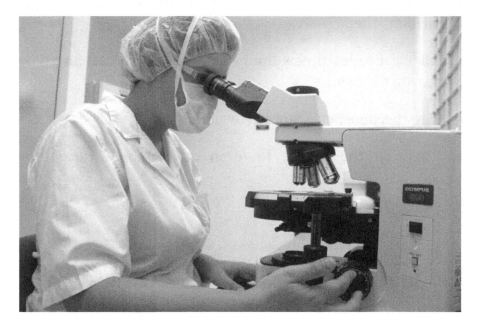

What is a Veterinary Technician?

Veterinary technicians make up a group in veterinary practice called "paraveterinary". These are people who assist a veterinary physician in the performance of their duties, or carry out animal health procedures autonomously as part of a veterinary care system.

They assist the vets but are placed higher than veterinary assistants in rank. They are able to perform more advanced tasks than veterinary assistants because, unlike the latter, their role requires that they are qualified. As such, veterinary technicians have to be qualified in the management and care of animals, laboratory work, clinical procedures and the processes of animal life.

To get a degree in this role, you have to apply for post-college education. On successful completion, you are awarded a bachelor or associate degree in veterinary technology. However, to keep their license and remain qualified for practice, veterinary technicians have to continue receiving education about their roles regularly and take veterinary exams. This is to enable them to perform up to the required standard in their job of assisting the vet and animal patients.

Veterinary technicians work with veterinarians in treating and diagnosing animals. They work in veterinary establishments such as zoos, animal hospitals, research centers, rescue facilities, clinics and animal laboratories. In these establishments, they make sure that animals are attended to and taken care of properly. They see to it that the technical part of veterinary procedures is up and running properly.

Simply put, a veterinary technician is a person who provides a vet and animal patients with proper technical care and support.

However, a veterinary technician is limited to certain duties. They cannot perform certain work which is outside the limitations set by the law of veterinary practice in their area. These laws could prohibit them from tasks such as drug prescription, diagnosis and anything involved with surgical processes.

Sometimes, veterinary technicians are used in place of veterinary technologists. Although both jobs have similarities, they are different job roles with different duties and qualifications.

As a result of their qualification, role and ranking, veterinary technicians are able to instruct and oversee assistants of their own. This means that they can supervise and give instructions to veterinary assistants.

How to become a Veterinary Technician

Since veterinary technicians are able to work on their own without being supervised and instructed by a veterinarian, their jobs requires that they are legally certified by a veterinary body. This certification may include any formal credentials they have relating to animal health and biology, and any other formal licenses of practice they have acquired. This legal certification, however, is not the same in every region.

In some regions where paraveterinary staff have job roles that are more advanced, the qualification requirements are based on both educational certification and practical experience. Anyone applying to be a veterinary technician must have the certification of a higher body of education.

The applicant must have a degree (bachelor or associate) from an institution of education which is legally recognized by moderating veterinary bodies such as the AVMA (American Veterinary Medical Association) or CVMA (Canadian Veterinary Medical Association).

The role of a veterinary technician is one that requires practical skills and experience. As such, to be a practitioner in the field they have to have good levels of practical experience after completing the academic program. This is to adequately prepare them for work.

In the course of gaining practical experience, the students are expected to maintain a report to document their experiences.

In other words, a logbook.

This report, however, is only considered authentic when validated and signed by a more senior professional supervising the student. The supervisor could be a veterinarian or another paraveterinary professional with a higher rank. The reason for a supervisor is to confirm the overall capabilities of the student and assess their ability to work under supervision and instructions.

In regards to this, the ruling body of veterinary practice in regions with more advanced paraveterinary practice might require other proof of practical experience like video records and data sheets. These requirements would be reviewed by the ruling body and checked for validity.

In other regions where the requirements to be a qualified veterinary technician are not so strict, another form of qualification can be used. In these places, only veterinary technicians who are registered to the regulatory bodies of veterinary practice are given the right to practice.

It is illegal in the United States for anyone who is not registered to identify and practice as a veterinary technician. They would be limited to only a few responsibilities in the field, and would not be able to carry out some tasks which other licensed vet technicians can do.

However, this limitation to licensing differs from one place to another. Other places might not permit an individual to practice at all without registration and licensing. The regulatory bodies responsible for managing this may have laws of their own. It is up to them to determine what level of education and qualifications are expected of anyone seeking to work as a veterinary technician. An example of a regulatory exam is the Veterinary Technician National Examination (VTNE).

In cases where veterinary technicians have advanced knowledge and skills about one or more fields of veterinary practice, they receive a different kind of qualification called "specialty certifications". This qualification is given in recognition of their expertise in fields such dentistry, critical care and emergencies, large animal medicine, anesthesiology, zoological medicine, wild veterinary nursing, exotic animal medicine, clinical pathology and practice and small animal medicine.

Veterinary technicians who fall into this category, and are qualified, get the tag Veterinary Technician Specialist (VTS). Their specific fields are further included in this tag.

Wow, that was a lot of technical information to digest! But it is important to know. Now let's look at the role of veterinary technician in more detail.

What Are the Duties of a Veterinary Technician?

The duties performed by a veterinary technician can depend on their place of work and the field of veterinary practice. However, they mostly always work alongside a veterinarian in caring for and treating animals.

The duties of vet technicians include a range of tasks such as laboratory work like collecting samples, clinical procedures like giving medications, and clerical services like documenting observations and writing reports. Other duties of veterinary technicians are listed below.

- It is the role of vet technicians to prepare animals to see the vet. They make sure the animals undergo veterinary procedures smoothly and without problems.

- Veterinary technicians take notes on animal patients for observation by collecting and maintaining their records for as long as the animals remain in veterinary care.

- While taking the notes of animals and maintaining their records, vet technicians observe animals closely and note any changes in them that might indicate how they react to the veterinary procedures given to them.

- In the case of an emergency, veterinary technicians are expected to provide animal patients with first aid treatments and nursing care until they are ready to see the vet.

- Since veterinary technicians provide technical support to vets, they are in charge of laboratory work that involves machines like x-rays, MRIs and ultrasounds. As such, they are responsible for taking the x-rays of animals and preparing the pictures.

- The qualifications of veterinary technicians make them capable of collecting samples from animals to test for diagnosis in laboratories. They then prepare reports and send them to the vet.

- Under the instructions of a vet, veterinary technicians can administer treatments and medication to animals.

- When animals are being treated or operated upon, it is the job of the veterinary technician to watch and record their activities and vitals so a comprehensive report can be prepared.

- Veterinary technicians also help veterinary doctors during the examination of animal patients to keep them calm and relaxed.

- Veterinary technicians are the ones who carry out dental procedures on animals in their care.

- Before the vet begins surgical procedures on an animal, the veterinary technician is expected to prepare the animal for the operation and ready all the machines needed by the vet.

- It is also their role to arrange surgical equipment and instruments, and stand by the vets to assist them during the surgery. They are meant to ensure that systems that support and monitor the animal are functional.

- When surgical procedures are being carried out on an animal, the veterinary technician is the one who administers the anesthesia according to the instructions of the vet. They are also to monitor the patients when anesthetized and make sure they don't wake mid-session.

- Veterinary technicians assist in clerical matters like managing the visiting clients, which are usually animal patients and their owners. They are to receive each client, assess the reason for their visit and then sort them in a particular order for the vet.

- Veterinary technicians are also able to perform some tasks in place of a vet, according to their qualifications. They could conduct small veterinary procedures like taking medical vitals, such as respiration and pulse rate, doing clinical services like cleaning and covering up injuries, performing psychological work like recuperation and abuse management.

- Veterinary technicians can do administrative duties in the organization. They can be in charge of taking inventory of purchases such as equipment, supplies, and pharmaceuticals.

- Also, in the role of administration, veterinary technicians are an important part of the relationship between clients and the organization. They are required to maintain relationships with the client and the organization so as to pass information correctly between both parties.

What Skills and Qualities Are Required From a Veterinary Technician?

Some of the skills required for the role of a veterinary technician include the following:

Human Relations

Even though the job of veterinary technician mainly involves taking care of animals, they have to be able to interact well with human clients and other members of the veterinary organization.

Good Listening Skills

The only way veterinary technicians are able to maintain the relationship between the clients, vets and organization is if they are able to listen to all parties and understand them. This skill helps the vet technicians connect better with the clients and report better to the vets. Also, it encourages teamwork between colleagues in the workplace.

Tidiness and Coordination

As a veterinary technician, you must be able to keep things organized and in working order. You are expected to be able to work with veterinary doctors and assistants. This means veterinary technicians have to be alert and co-ordinated.

Good Communication Skills

A veterinary technician must be able to relay information from the vets to clients and vice versa. This skill also helps the veterinary technicians better relate with and instruct veterinary assistants.

Smartness and Speed

The job of a veterinary technician involves being sound intellectually and quick to act. You should be able to produce practical solutions to problems and work quickly to avoid delays.

Mental Alertness

Veterinary technicians must have the mental ability to make the best choices for animals, as their lives might depend on quick and thorough decision making.

Observation Skills

A veterinary technician must be able to note changes quickly in the state of an animal's health.

Chapter 10

Ancient & Modern Veterinary Practices

Ancient Veterinary Practices

As you can imagine, the care for animals in prehistoric and medieval times was quite different to what is available today. Back in the day, veterinarians were called mule, cattle or donkey doctors. This was mainly because the practice of animal medicine revolved around livestock and "beasts of burden".

There were little to no animals put aside as pets. In fact, animals that achieved pet status were often nothing more than farm animals that were kept in the home for specific purposes such as dairy and egg production.

Since these animals were not sold for profit and lived with their owners until their final stages of life, they were considered pets — or something close to that.

Like all living things, these animals would fall sick sometimes. Owners, not wanting to lose their animals, sought out means of curing their ailments. The treatments available in the ancient era were as limited as their technology and their knowledge of animals. While some of these veterinary practices worked on some animals, they caused more harm than good among others.

Some ancient veterinary practices include:

Bloodletting

Bloodletting in ancient times involved the practice of withdrawing blood from an ailing animal in order to cure or prevent ailments. Ancient doctors believed diseases and sicknesses originated from bad blood clogged up in the veins.

This belief originated from the limited knowledge available to the ancient medical system, which stated that blood could be used up, and that the arteries sometimes contained air rather than blood. The ancients knew nothing about blood circulation at the time, believing blood to be a bodily fluid that could be exhausted.

The ancient Greeks and Romans saw bodily fluids as what they termed "humors". Within the bounds of their knowledge, they believed that bodily fluids were responsible for temperaments. As such, a cranky animal could be diagnosed as having too little or an excess amount of blood in its body.

When a later discovery of arteries showed they contained blood and not air, bloodletting was seen as a means of achieving "humoral balance". The ancients considered all living things to have a measure of four humors which were responsible for their state of health. These four humors were black bile, phlegm, yellow bile and blood.

The process of bloodletting thrived because the ancient medical system recommended that bodily fluids, inclusive of the four humors, were to be kept at specific levels to ensure perfect health. Hence, any increase in one of these bodily fluids was seen as the cause of disease and should thus be drained to the correct level.

Another source of bloodletting as a means of curing animal diseases is of Egyptian origin. The ancient Egyptians mistook the red-colored perspiration of the hippo to be a healing technique. They believed the hippo scratched itself and drew blood to relieve itself of distress and ailments. This knowledge contributed to the belief in bloodletting as a form of reducing and easing problems in animals.

The weirder part of bloodletting is the instruments used in draining these humors. Ancient veterinary practices encouraged the use of leeches in bloodletting. The sick animal was introduced to a number of leeches, which preyed on its blood until the desired level of blood volume was reached.

This method was effective in reducing sicknesses connected to high blood pressure since blood volume was reduced; but on the whole, it was more harmful than beneficial because it encouraged parasitism. There also was the danger of contracting other infections due to this crude method.

The practice of bloodletting in veterinary medicine was not stopped until the late 19th century.

Acupuncture

Acupuncture in veterinary practice is the use of fine needles on animals as a means of relieving pain and curing certain ailments. The needles are inserted into specific points of the body of animals to tweak their neural response to pain and other sicknesses, which is then meant to result in healing effects.

Acupuncture on animals can be traced to the ancient practices of healing done by the Chinese thousands of years ago. This practice was a result of the popularity of a legend which claimed that horses lame in their legs regained use of their legs when arrows hit them at certain points during battle. With no thorough thought given to the morality of this legend, acupuncture was carried out on animals in ancient times.

History has it that in China, persons in charge of the chariots of war were called "horse priests". These people popularized the practice of veterinary acupuncture as a method of healing. The practice would later evolve to be used as a means of preventing future problems in animals, especially horses and other beasts of war, since they were very important in these times. Veterinary acupuncture was used as a protection and cure against conditions such as lameness, colic and sprains.

Research has shown that veterinary acupuncture in ancient times was in no way similar to present-day acupuncture. This is because the ancient Chinese texts termed the practice of animal veterinary acupuncture "zhen". This term was then roughly translated to mean acupuncture, but reading these texts further showed it implied something else.

As such, ancient veterinary acupuncture included other crude methods of treatment that didn't involve the use of needles alone. The needles were simply instruments used for cauterization, surgery and amputations, and bloodletting in place of leeches. Since the belief in humors and humoral levels was widely popular in ancient times, this can be accepted as the truth of ancient veterinary acupuncture.

Cauterization

Cauterization in veterinary practice is sealing or cutting off body tissue of an animal by the use of extremely hot or cold instruments.

In ancient times, cauterization in veterinary practice mainly involved burning a part of an animal's body as a means of closing up or cutting off the particular part. Due to the unavailability of antibiotics and proper surgical procedures in ancient times, certain conditions in animals like infections, undesired external growths, and bleeding, were contained and treated by cauterization. The animals were put through a crude, painful process similar to branding as a means of curing them of such medical conditions.

The ancients believed the extreme temperatures used could contain bodily damage and bleeding in animals by destroying certain tissue. This further prompted the use of cauterization in removing external growths on animals since it could be used to contain any ruptures that might occur. Also, the heat was believed to kill possible infections that could affect the animals through their injuries.

Whilst that was a widely held belief, modern-day medicine holds that ancient cauterization made an animal more prone to infections because of the damage done to its body.

Primarily, the ancients used cauterization after surgical procedures on animals to treat wounds and prevent inflammation. It served as an early alternative before the advent of antibiotics. The ancients used it as a method to cover up bloodletting holes, hemorrhages and amputations.

Cauterization in ancient times was done by heating a piece of metal over a flame. The heated metal could be the blade of a knife or lance. When the material was heated to a red glow, it was then applied to the affected body part. The heat of the material seared the skin of the affected part, causing the blood and tissues to heat up. This process makes blood coagulation faster by producing blisters which contain the bleeding, even though major damage would be done to the tissues themselves. In other cases of application, the heated material is used to cut off an external growth.

Medieval times saw cauterization in veterinary practice evolve to include the treatment of dental problems in animals. Cauterization was used by medieval vets to remove a decaying or aching tooth and provide relief to animals. Also, in ancient practices such as circumcision and castration, cauterization was used to help control bleeding and prevent infections.

Castration

Castration is the process of removing some part or parts of the reproductive organs of animals, especially male animals.

As mentioned earlier, people kept animals for specific purposes in previous times. These animals served two major purposes, production and labor. The animals meant for production were cared for differently than the animals kept for work. The former were regarded as livestock and the latter as beasts of burden.

Both classes of animals were of economic value to people in ancient times, which was why they sought ways of keeping them healthy and improving their quality of life. One such method was castration. Castration in ancient veterinary practice involved the removal of the testicles. The reasons for this included fattening the animal, reducing reproductive urges and improving behavioral traits by lowering aggression.

People back then discovered that removing the testicles of an animal made its meat taste better, made it grow bigger and stronger in build and gave it better market appeal. As such, they applied veterinary measures to castrate some of their animals.

Hence, the practice of castration in ancient times was mainly to fatten beasts of burden and make them strong for work or to improve the taste and volume of meat. Castration was done especially on horses and cattle. Since there was no anesthesia and these animals put up a fight when hurt, castration in ancient times was a long, crude and dangerous process for all concerned.

Modern Veterinary Practices

In modern times, the advance of technology and improved knowledge of animals has given rise to much better veterinary practices. These practices are far less crude and safeguard the lives of animals and ensure their wellbeing.

Examples of modern veterinary practices include:

Detection of microfractures

Animals, pets, livestock and working animals in modern times face many risks of bone problems. These animals are likely to develop microscopic fractures in their bones from being put to use or just going about their daily activities. These fractures, although unnoticeable at first, can become complex bone fractures over time or grow to become terminal. Hence, vets have seen the need to treat and prevent this occurrence early.

Modern vets have adopted the practice of detecting the presence of microfractures in the bones of animals by identifying the sonic waves they produce. This has helped to contain and reduce the damage from fractures by ensuring early detection.

Magnetic resonance imaging (MRI)

Another common modern veterinary practice is magnetic resonance imaging or MRI. Vets use MRI machines to scan and study the brains of animals. The results of the scan are then used to better treat the animal or prevent the worsening of its health.

The use of MRI in veterinary practice is not limited to scanning or studying the brain. It can also be used for scanning the structure of tissue before surgery. This makes the vet better prepared for any surgical procedure to be done on the animal and reduces the risk of errors.

3D modeling

In modern times, veterinary medicine requires vets to have a good knowledge of animals before taking any medical action. In order to meet this requirement and better understand the body structure of animals, veterinary medicine has employed the practice of 3D modeling.

Three-dimensional versions of the animals or specific body parts are prototyped. These prototypes are made to be identical to the original features of the animals as seen in scan results. This practice makes it easy for vets to understand the body structure of the animals and to know the best medical solutions to their problems.

Also, vets can use 3D modeling as a teaching aid when educating the owners of these animals on how to better care for them.

Laparoscopic surgery

Unlike ancient times, when surgery was done on animals with little to no knowledge of the structure of their bodies, modern-day veterinary practice ensures detailed knowledge of the animal before surgery.

In achieving this, vets use a laparoscope to observe the internal structure of an animal before commencing surgical procedures. A laparoscope is a thin camera device inserted into the hollow organs of an animal through an incision in its abdomen or thorax (chest).

The laparoscope shows a clear image of the insides of the animal and enables vets to plan their surgical procedures to avoid errors.

Chapter 11

Myths & Fun Facts About Veterinary Medicine

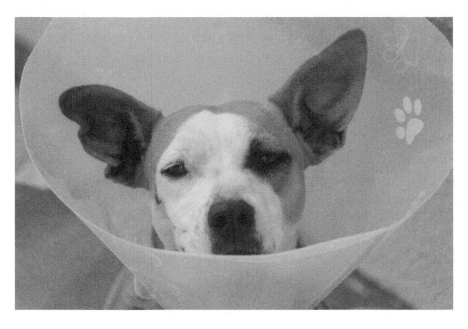

Veterinary Myths

Like all professions, veterinary medicine is not without its myths.

The myths of veterinary medicine are the common beliefs held about the practice which are often exaggerated or invented forms of the truth. Some myths surrounding the veterinary profession include:

Veterinary medicine is a male profession

The profession of veterinary medicine has long been plagued by this myth. However, it is clearly untrue. Veterinary medicine is open to both males and females, and both genders are given equal opportunities in the practice.

This myth must have risen from the early years when veterinary practice consisted mostly of males. However, recent research has shown that the rate of females becoming vets has increased in recent times. Although some areas of the field still remain mainly populated by males, the female population in veterinary practice continues to rise. This debunks the myth of veterinary medicine being a male-oriented practice.

Veterinarians don't qualify as doctors

Just because this branch of medicine deals with animals doesn't make its practitioners lesser compared to doctors of other branches of medicine. In fact, they are just as important and equal to other doctors because they are masters of their field just like the others.

Vets go through a medical program for four years to earn a doctorate degree. The DMV — Doctorate in Veterinary Medicine — is then awarded to them when they successfully complete the course. This degree is similar to those of doctors in other fields: as such, veterinarians are just as much doctors as other medics.

Also, vets can arguably be described as the most widely experienced of the many fields of medicine. This is because veterinarians are taught to treat many different species of animals. This makes them more specialized than doctors in other fields of medicine, who only have a skill set that is applicable to humans.

Veterinarians can choose to work as animal consultants, professional teachers, animal researchers, military servicemen, regulatory workers for government or as corporate employers or employees.

Veterinary medicine is mainly for smaller, household pets

This myth could easily be the most popular of the lot. However, it is untrue. It is correct that a significant amount of animal patients veterinarians receive and treat are pets, but this does not entirely sum up the expertise of the practice.

Also, the animals which veterinarians care for aren't always small or household based. Vets are equipped to treat animals of different sizes and habitats. The animals could be of the domesticated or wild sort, small or large, and would still be treated by a vet.

This is because all vets are taught to care for animals irrespective of their classifications. Just because many vets base their practice in areas relating to pets or smaller animals doesn't make the profession entirely limited to that class of animals. To further prove this point, below is a list of disciplines in veterinary medicine that covers the different classes of animals.

Large Animal Medicine: As its name explains, this discipline focuses on vets who treat and care for especially large animals.

Equine Animal Medicine: This discipline of veterinary medicine deals with horses alone.

Mixed Practice Medicine: This discipline deals with a much wider range of animals rather than a particular type.

These disciplines and others show that veterinary medicine encompasses the care and treatment of all animals — great and small.

You cannot study veterinary medicine without a pre-vet degree

This myth has kept many people from choosing veterinary medicine. But, as with the other myths, it is untrue. Veterinary medicine, like other medical fields, doesn't necessarily require an applicant to have studied any animal-related courses such as biology, animal science, pre-vet, zoology, etc.

Although a qualification in any of these subjects could greatly help an applicant because they teach similar material to veterinary medicine, it is not a compulsory prerequisite. Applicants can apply for any field of veterinary medicine of their choice so long as they have the necessary grades required.

Fun Facts About Veterinary Medicine

Below are some fun facts about veterinary medicine that might just leave you wowed.

- Some animals are quite secretive when birthing their young, so sometimes, even their owners are denied this thrilling experience. Vets, however, have the privilege of helping animals deliver their young and keeping them healthy.

- Veterinarians are professionals with many different skill sets. This gives them an edge over a general practitioner in the medical field. Vets can work as counselors, surgeons, oncologists, radiologists, psychiatrists, nutritionists for animals.

- Veterinarians almost always never get tired of their jobs because they get to meet new animals regularly, which rekindles their love for the job.

- In veterinary practice, dogs are the most common animal patients. More proof that they are indeed man's best friend.

- The word "veterinary" has disputed roots; many languages have root words similar to it in meaning. However, Latin is credited with being the origin language of the word "veterinarian" since it comes from the Latin root word "veterinae", which means "working animals" or "beasts of burden".

- Early veterinary medicine was mainly practiced on beasts of burden and livestock since animals were seldom ever kept as pets.

- The most common field in veterinary medicine is the discipline of general household pets. However, every veterinary practitioner has a specific field of practice.

- Knowledge of veterinary medicine is sometimes applied to solve specific problems in humans. This is because about 61% of the agents that cause diseases in human beings are produced by animals.

- There are vets who don't practice their profession on animals. Instead, they dedicate their time to developing new sources of treatments and doing research.

- Veterinary medicine is arguably the only field of medicine that can be practiced on a more frugal level. Since their patients are mainly animals, vets don't have to keep up with newer and more expensive trends in medical equipment. They can simply use refurbished or used equipment, which is purchased at cheaper rates.

- Vets take two oaths upon completing their degree. On the first oath, they are to swear to put their knowledge of animals to use in helping to care and protect their wellbeing and health. On the second, they promise to abide by the ethics of the veterinary industry, continue the practice in dignity, ease the suffering of animals, improve the health of the public and promote the knowledge of animal medicine.

- As fun as the profession can be for animal lovers, vets face certain dangers while performing their jobs. This is because there is no accurate way of predicting the behavior or response of an animal to medical procedures. This, in turn, makes the vet liable to different work hazards.

- In ancient times, veterinary practitioners were not called veterinarians or vets as we know them now. They were called different names based on the type of animals they treated. For example, mule doctors were called "mulomedicus", horse doctors "hippiatroi", and livestock doctors "medicuspecuarius".

- The earliest recorded use of the term "veterinary medicine" was in an ancient Egyptian text called the *Papyrus of*

Kahun in the year 1800 B.C. The second reported use of the term appeared in the text titled *Code of Hammurabi in* 1754 B.C.

- There is a debate on who the founding father of veterinary medicine is. Many schools of thought have come up with three different ancients to whom the title can be attributed: Galen, Hippocrates and Vegetius. Of the three, however, Vegetius is the generally accepted one given his title of "father of veterinary medicine".

- The people of ancient times began taking care of animals before their fellow humans. That is, the practice of veterinary medicine might already have been established by our ancestors before human medication.

- Following the domestication of animals in ancient times, there were many outbreaks of diseases caused by the closeness of humans and animals. This marked the beginning of cross-species veterinary practice because ancient people sought ways to cure these diseases.

- The earliest practitioners of veterinary medicine were herdsmen and shepherds because they were believed to have more knowledge about animals.

- Before any knowledge of animals existed in ancient times, veterinary practice on sick animals involved the use of magic, faith healing, sacrifices and incantations.

- France boasts having first established a college dedicated to the study of veterinary medicine in the year 1762 in Lyons.

- The first ever graduate of veterinary medicine to practice his profession in America was a man named Charles Clark in the year 1817.

- For people who love animals, studying veterinary medicine is one way to live your dream, as vets spend their days around animals. Imagine "going to work" meaning being around animals you love. Beautiful!

Chapter 12

Pioneering Veterinarians

Sometimes, we must look to the past in order to keep moving forward. The lives of those who laid the groundwork for what we can now call a profession are an inspiration. We can learn from these individuals that our struggles, fears and hopes are not so new.

In fact, they had fewer resource than we now enjoy. Yet, they were able to make the giant strides they are now acclaimed for. We also learn from them that success does not play favorites. It is not a respecter of wealth or race. All that it demands is an unquenchable passion and a willingness to work hard.

The men and women listed below are from widely different

parts of the world and possess varying levels of academic qualifications. Some found it much easier to achieve their goals than others, but they all left their mark on veterinary medicine.

They went out on a limb to better the field of animal science, and we cannot be more thankful for their pioneering efforts. Animals all over the world, who have benefited in any way from the skills of a veterinarian, are living better lives because of their efforts.

Can you guess what you have in common with these vets of old? Yes, a love and compassion for animals and an interest in veterinary medicine. If they were able, despite the many odds, to make their mark on veterinary medicine, then you can too. I believe that you can.

So, let us celebrate these heroes. I hope the men and women listed below offer you inspiration.

Claude Bourgelat

Born in France in the year 1712, Claude was the son of Charles Pierre Bourgelat and Genevieve Terrasson. Although Claude started off being the son of a wealthy father, this did not last very long. Legal issues over some of his father's estates led to a fall in his social class. He was not poor, but he was far from rich.

This did not deter Claude. He studied to be a lawyer and practiced for about seven years; during this time, he formed close relationships with influential people. He also proved to be an excellent horse rider, which got him the attention and recognition of the king.

As his interest in animal science grew, he started researching the physiology, hygiene and anatomy of horses. This he did with the help of two of his educated friends, Claude Ponteau and Jean-Baptiste Charmetton, who were surgeons for humans. He also wrote many books that made him popular among the science community of his time.

He then began to envision a school where animal science could be studied for the improvement of livestock productivity. On the 4th of August 1761, he was permitted by the king's council to open a veterinary school in Lyon, which was the first of its kind anywhere in the world.

Students learned about livestock diseases, and the ways in which they can be cured. Individuals from all over the world came to study at this unique school, and they left inspired to recreate similar institutions in their own countries. In his lifetime, Claude would go on to establish another veterinary school in Alfort.

It is for these reasons that Claude Bourgelat is considered, by some, to be the father of modern veterinary science.

Bernhard Lauritz Frederik Bang

Jacob Henrik Bang wedded Louise Marie Josephine Mott in 1848 and they had a son. A boy who would go on to become a popular and influential figure in the field of veterinary medicine in Denmark, having several medical eponyms (medical terms that were named after him) to his credit.

One of the things Bernhard Lauritz Frederik Bang is acclaimed for is his method for applying antiseptics during animal surgery. Up until he started doing this, antiseptics were only used for human surgery. Lack of antiseptic was one of the reasons for many unsuccessful animal surgeries.

Bang would also become a professor at the Royal Veterinary and Agricultural College in the year 1880. He taught pathological anatomy and the methods of applying antiseptics during animal surgery.

It was Bang who discovered what caused cattle to lose their babies and why it was contagious to other cattle. The culprit in the bodies of cattle responsible for this was named Brucella abortus. Brucellosis, which causes fever in humans, is sometimes called Bang's Disease.

A notable figure in his time and honored years after that, Bang died on June 22, 1932, just two weeks after his birthday.

Arnold Theiler

If you were born in Switzerland in the 19th century, it was almost inevitable that you would grow up and join the many others in the country championing the progress of science. This was the place and time into which Arnold Theiler was born. He was born to Franz and Maria Theiler on the 26th of March, 1867.

The rise of scientific study which characterized this era meant that Arnold would, ultimately, become a scientist himself. It was much the same as technology and social media is to us today. Some of his earliest influences in the field of science were his teachers. They included F. Mühleberg and his father, who was a science teacher at a school in Frick.

Like many veterinarians, Arnold had to further his education at university, where he found comparative anatomist A. Lang, professor of veterinary pathology and anatomy E. Zschokke, and genial botanist H. Schinz. These scientists, in no small way, stoked the flames of wonder and curiosity for the workings of nature in young Arnold.

After graduating and being certified to practice as a vet, things weren't easy for him. Being unsatisfied with his small village practice and wanting to experience the larger world, he set his sights on South Africa. Emma Sophie Jegge, whom he married in 1893, believed so much in his dream of becoming a world-acclaimed veterinarian, that she sponsored his voyage to South Africa.

Things were not rosy over there either; he had to live through a war. But he established a name for himself, helping South African farmers combat the diseases that plagued their animals, and relating with them on a personal level. He achieved a great deal in the field of biological veterinary. So much that, after his death in 1936, a statue was made in his honor in South Africa.

Aleen Cust

Until fairly recently, veterinary medicine and other science-heavy fields were dominated by men. Women had to fight constantly against the odds for the right to work, and many just gave up in the end.

Aleen Cust was not among those.

As far as Ireland and Britain were concerned, she became the very first female veterinarian. After her nurse training at London Hospital, she decided to go to veterinary school. This was when her family pushed against her. Being of aristocratic descent, it would have been considered embarrassing that a woman from their family was seen studying to be a vet.

She found a way around this though. With the encouragement of her guardian, she used an alias, A.I. Custance, to get into New Veterinary College, Edinburgh.

Still, this did not mean there were no more barriers before her. The Royal Council of Veterinary Surgeons was opposed to her becoming a member of their society. For this reason, she had no formal right to practice as a veterinary surgeon. She tried to have this overturned, but was initially unsuccessful. On the 21st of December 1922, after the Sex Disqualification Act had been passed into law, she was allowed to sit for her final exams and was given her diploma. Her years of struggle and defiance of the patriarchal system had paid off.

This victory, unfortunately, came a little too late. Her health was fast deteriorating, and she only had the strength to practice for two more years. She sold her clinic and moved to a new home in Hampshire, England. Aleen died in Jamaica on the 29th of January, 1937. The cause of her death was heart failure.

One of her legacies was the Aleen Cust Research Scholarship, which offers scholarships mainly to women to do great things in veterinary science. This legacy still stands today.

Isabelle Bruce Reid

While Aleen Cust was the first female vet in Ireland and Britain, other women were conquering their respective countries as well.

In Australia, it was Isabelle Bruce Reid. She was born on the 21st of December, 1883, to Robert Reid and Mary Jane Clancy. She became interested in caring for animals when she was a child tending to her father's horses, but she did not want to be a vet at first. She wanted to be a singer, but had to give it up because it did not sit well with her parents. They thought it was not proper for someone of her social standing — her father was a wealthy politician.

So, she chose her next favorite thing to do — caring for animals.

Isabelle secured a place at Melbourne Veterinary College in 1902. She completed the course four years later, and was the only one of five students to pass the final-year exams. Immediately after, she began practicing as a certified vet. This lasted until she retired in 1923. Until her death in 1945, she continued to train, breed and care for animals.

The Belle Bruce Reid Award is given to female veterinarians who have made notable achievements in the field of veterinary science.

James Alfred Wight

If you ask your parents, they might have a few good things to say about this man. He showed just how fun being a vet could be. Some of his books were adapted for TV, and they depicted humans in harmony with their animals. He was born in Sunderland, England, on the 3rd of October 1916. His parents were James Henry Wight and Hannah Bell Wight. Both his parents were musically inclined, so you would have expected the junior James to be a musician.

Instead, he had two great passions in his life: football and veterinary medicine. He attended Glasgow Veterinary School and graduated in 1939. Less than a year after, in January 1940, James was practicing his passion.

He chose a pen name for the books he wrote, because of a ban on veterinarians showcasing their services in that manner. Fortunately, this is not the case anymore. He used James Herriot for himself and Helen Alderson for his wife. That James even began writing books was all thanks to his wife. When he was 50, his wife convinced him that it was long overdue and talked to him about putting down his experiences and ideas in writing.

At first, he did not write about animals. Instead, he chose to talk about football, but got rejected a few times by publishers. Finally, he decided to write books that enlightened people about veterinary science by telling stories of his experiences. This time, he not only got accepted by a publishing company, but also became a famous writer. Books such as *If Only They Could Talk* and *All Creatures Great and Small* were published to national and world acclaim.

In 1979, he was honored with a doctorate by Heriot-Watt University, although it was attributed to his pen name. He died in 1995 after four years of battling cancer.

Jean-Marie Camille Guérin

Jean-Marie Camille Guérin was born in France on the 22nd of December 1872. At the tender age of ten, Jean-Marie lost his father to tuberculosis. This may have led to his interest in the field of medicine, but I cannot say that for certain. He did contribute incredibly towards the creation of vaccines against tuberculosis in humans and animals.

He was closely affiliated with Albert Calmette. They both worked together to develop a vaccine against tuberculosis called Bacillus Calmette-Guérin or BCG.

In 1892, he attended the National Veterinary School of Alfort, otherwise called École Nationale Vétérinaire d'Alfort in French. He joined the Pasteur Institute of Lille five years later, where he met someone who would turn out to be very instrumental to certain successes in his life.

This person was the bacteriologist Albert Calmette. Jean-Marie worked for a while as his technician, but rose in the institute to handle even more important tasks. It was as the head of the laboratory that he began to research a vaccine for tuberculosis.

The success of this led to more job promotions and national recognition. One of the highest positions that was trusted to Jean-Marie was president of the Veterinary Academy of France in 1949. He was awarded the Scientific Grand Prix by the French Academy Of Sciences. The fruition of Guérin and Calmette's work was and still is beneficial to both humans and animals.

On the 9th of June 1961, Jean-Marie Camille Guérin died at the respectable old age of 89.

Suzanne Morrow Francis

How about a vet who was also an Olympian? Suzanne competed in the 1952 Olympics as a figure skater. Earlier, in 1948, she had won the bronze medal with Wallace Diestelmeyer. Despite her presence in the Winter Olympics of 1952, Suzanne graduated from Ontario Veterinary College in Canada with her diploma.

Of all the vets mentioned in this chapter, it could be said that no one loved animals as much as she did. Dogs were her favorite. Even more specificly, German Shepherds were the dogs closest to her heart. She could often be seen with a dog by her side, everywhere she went.

In figure skating, Suzanne is credited, alongside Wallace Diestelmeyer, with being the first person to perform the death spiral — a circular move in which the male lowers his partner to the ice while she is arched backwards gliding on one foot. She is as respected in the world of sports as she is in the field of veterinary medicine.

You can look to the life of Suzanne Morrow Francis as proof that you can live your life to the fullest. Working towards being a veterinarian does not mean you have to give up all of your other dreams. It only means you have to think of a way to work around your studies without compromising your chances of graduating from veterinary school. Suzanne proved that this is not only possibile, but that you can thrive while doing so.

She died on June 11, 2006, at the age of 75. Her life was and will always be an inspiration.

Alfreda Johnson Webb

It is a wonderful thing that both genders are represented in veterinary medicine. Yet, as I am sure you know, skin color is just as important too for equality. It is liberating when people of all races are given the opportunity to try their hand at any profession. Alfreda Johnson Webb was the first African-American woman to graduate with a doctorate in veterinary medicine in 1949 and, consequentially, the first African-American woman to practice this profession.

She was a member of the planning committee in the establishment of a veterinary school at North Carolina University. This would come to fruition in 1981. In the same school, she served as a professor of biology and laboratory animal science. You may be able to tell by now that her influence was far-reaching indeed.

Her doctorate and practice were not the only records she broke in her lifetime. In 1972, she became the first African-American woman in the North Carolina General Assembly. This is more proof that you can be a vet and still live out your other passions. She was recognized and awarded by her sorority for her excellence in politics. In 1999, she was inducted into the agriculture hall of fame of North Carolina University.

Alfreda Johnson Webb died on the 14th of October in 1992, but lives forever in the hearts of countless veterinarians who strive to achieve their goals despite the odds.

William Llewelyn Lloyd-Jones

More popularly known as Buster, William was born in London in 1914 — a time associated with the First World War. Buster was the personification of a veterinarian who cared for all animals great and small. During the war, he made it his duty to care for animals that had been affected by the constant fighting and neglect.

Animals are usually considered the least important living things during such crisis situations, but not to Buster. He kept a colorful variety of these animals. Whenever he would find an injured or sick animal, it was unlike Buster to walk on by without offering aid.

An impressive number of species of birds, cats, dogs, monkeys and reptiles were represented in Buster's home. Besides this, people left their animals with Buster for reasons that ranged from having been drafted to just not being financially capable of caring for them.

After the war, many of these people would not take their animals back. Still, Buster was not discouraged by this. He continued to care for them regardless. He not only cared for and played with the animals, but he also observed them. He said of animals in his book *The Animals Came in One by One* that they have an "instinctive wisdom" and a "deeply ingrained understanding of nature".

His time with animals led him to discover several herbal remedies that could be used to treat some of their illnesses. This eventually gave him a business idea which would grow to be Denes, a veterinary company for herbal medicines.

Did you know that Sir Winston Churchill was a regular client of Buster's? People of different classes brought their pets to him because of his skill, experience and the love he infused into his practice. Even though Buster Lloyd-Jones has been dead since 1980, Denes still continues to thrive in today's world.

Louis J. Camuti

Are you a cat lover? If you are, then you and Dr Camuti would have made really good friends. As far as the history of veterinary medicine in America goes, Louis J. Camuti was the first man to focus his veterinary practice on cats alone.

He was born in Italy on the 30th of August 1893. Camuti told a story of how a cat had saved him from dying when he was eleven, sick with a fever and in a burning house. The cat had jumped on his bed to rouse him fully awake so he could recognize the danger and escape. He then got the rest of his family safely outside.

This could have led to his choice of a veterinary career focused on cats. He was also known to make house calls instead of waiting in a clinic for patients to visit. This meant an even busier practice, but he did not mind. He enjoyed it, in fact. One of his quotes goes: "There is something about the presence of a cat that seems to take the bite out of being alone."

Do you agree with that, or do you think it's true for a different animal?

On the 24th of February 1981, as he went to treat a cat, Louis J. Camuti died of a heart attack.

Sophia Yin

Sophia believed in positive reinforcement as an effective method for training animals, and she became famous for this. Do you know what positive reinforcement means?

You probably already use this method on your animals. This is when you reward your pets, livestock or working animals for their good behavior, but hold back when the animals behave badly. It is a much better, effective and humane solution to training animals than beating or screaming at them.

Sophia made videos, wrote several books and ran a veterinary practice which encouraged her clients to utilize positive reinforcement. Like you, she had wanted to be a vet ever since she was a little child.

Sophia Yin was born in 1966 and got into the University of California, Davis, in 1989. Upon graduating four years after with a doctorate in veterinary medicine, she put the bulk of her efforts into teaching pet owners about animal behavior. It really is sad to know that many healthy animals get euthanized simply because their owners find it difficult to train them.

Sophia thought so too. To solve this, she gathered highly scientific information on conditioning and animal behavior, but presented it in an easy-to-understand format. Fewer pets got yelled at, beaten or killed for their "unfathomable" or "uncontrollable" behavior because of Sophia's hard work. Her educational videos were not only useful to pet owners, but to veterinary assistants and other groups who have to work closely with animals to improve their well-being.

If you ever write a book concerning animals, you could try to pitch it to her publishing company called CattleDog Publishing.

There are so many wonderful things to say about this awesome veterinarian. She enlightened people and brought happiness to pet owners and their animals. She died on the 28th of September 2014.

Conclusion

These wonderful people you have just read about bring us to the end of this book. Did you enjoy reading about them? It is reassuring and enlightening to hear about people who have succeeded in the path you are hoping to follow. It frees the mind from worrying about the unknown and inspires courage. Now you know that aspiring to be a veterinarian is not an impossible dream. If they did it, often from very challenging backgrounds, so can you.

If you are able to, find a practicing veterinarian who is willing to be your mentor and let their wisdom and experience be your stepping stone to success. Fortunately, there is no shortage of vets who are happy to encourage young people, like yourself, on their way to achieving their dreams.

Veterinarians have done a lot to educate people about animal behavior, but not every person in the world has been receptive to this. There are a lot of people who are unkind to their animals because they simply do not understand them. Remember, as a vet you can do as much good, if not more, by spreading knowledge as well as treating animals.

Make no mistake, learning veterinary medicine takes up a lot of time and demands commitment and great attention. However, having a mentor and deep passion for helping animals will help you stay the course.

In this book, I have strived to be honest and realistic with you about the work involved. But never forget, if you love animals and being a vet is your true calling in life, you will enjoy every minute of it. The work involved will seem like a privilege rather than a burden.

Also, keep in mind that if you have other interests you need not drop them completely. All you have to work out is how to properly and wisely manage your time. Many animal doctors have been in similar situations and juggled both passions.

So you don't have to give up your other interests. There's always a way to work around them. Remember Suzanne and Alfreda? Well, there are many other stories just like theirs. Many vets in the past, and currently, have been able to strike a balance between veterinary medicine and their other passions. You can too.

Veterinarians find their jobs fun, touching and enlightening. Most of them would never want to do anything else. Most days come with ups, down, thrills and the unpredictable, but usually end on a fulfilling note. Leading to fulfilling life.

I wish you every success on your path forward and hope this book has served to show you what being a vet — and becoming one — is truly like.

Susanna Lee

The Veterinarian's Oath

When you become a vet, here is what you will have to agree to abide by - *The Veterinarian's Oath*. There is no better way to end this book than by reciting it. Read it through now and let the words inspire you to move forward with your heroic career path.

> *Being admitted to the profession of veterinary medicine, I solemnly swear to use my scientific knowledge and skills for the benefit of society through the protection of animal health and welfare, the prevention and relief of animal suffering, the conservation of animal resources, the promotion of public health, and the advancement of medical knowledge.*
>
> *I will practice my profession conscientiously, with dignity, and in keeping with the principles of veterinary medical ethics. I accept as a lifelong obligation the continual improvement of my professional knowledge and competence.*

Notable Colleges for Veterinary Medicine

You cannot be a veterinarian without first going to college. The colleges listed below are some of the best, and oldest, in the world. Keep them in mind for when you make your applications.

Colorado State University

This school was founded in 1870.

Location: Fort Collins, Colorado, US.

Veterinary program began in 1907.

The tuition fee for this school is $60,152 for unsponsored students and $36,220 for sponsored students.

University of California, Davis

This school was founded in 1905.

Location: Davis, California, US.

Veterinary program began in 1946.

The tuition fee for this school is $11,442 per year. Non-residents of California, such as international students, would pay an additional $12,245.

Texas A&M University

This school was founded in 1871.

Location: College Station, Texas, US.

Veterinary program began in 1916.

The tuition fee for this school is $24,160 per year for residents of Texas and $37,164 for non-residents.

Royal Veterinary College

This school was founded in 1791.

Location: Royal College St, London, UK.

Veterinary program began in 1791.

The tuition fee for this school is £9,250 per year.

University of Glasgow

This school was founded in 1451.

Location: University Avenue, Glasgow, Scotland, UK.

Veterinary program began in 1862.

The tuition fee for this school is £45,170.

Utrecht University

This school was founded in 1636.

Location: Utrecht, Netherlands.

Veterinary program began in 1925.

The tuition fee for this school is €16,600 per year for non-EU nationals and €2,083 for Dutch, Swiss and other citizens of the EU.

The University of Sydney

This school was founded in 1850.

Location: Camperdown, Sydney, Australia.

Veterinary program began in 1910.

The tuition fee for this school is A$10,958 per year for Australian citizens and A$49,500 for international students.

University of Ghent

This school was founded in 1817.

Location: St. Pietersnieuwstraat, Ghent, Belgium.

Veterinary program began in 1933.

The tuition fee for this school is €938.80 per year.

Massey University

This school was founded in 1927.

Location: Palmerston North, New Zealand.

Veterinary program began in 1963.

The tuition fee for this school is NZ$12,307.20 per year.

University of Veterinary Medicine, Vienna

This school was founded in 1767.

Location: Vienna, Austria.

Veterinary program began in 1767.

The tuition fee for this school is €909.70 per year.

Iowa State University

This school was founded in 1858.

Location: Iowa, US.

Veterinary program began in 1879.

The tuition fee for this school is $24,536 for residents in the United States and $52,502 for non-residents.

*The tuition fees listed are up-to-date at the time of writing this book. However, they are subject to change at any time.

Made in the USA
Middletown, DE
19 August 2020

16070533R00070